T0365597

A GATEWAY TO SUCCESS!

Fast Track
to success

A science/formula for achieving
a career you deserve

KAREN MELONIE GOULD

authorHOUSE®

AuthorHouse™
1663 Liberty Drive
Bloomington, IN 47403
www.authorhouse.com
Phone: 1-800-839-8640

Published by AuthorHouse 11/09/2013

ISBN: 978-1-4918-8431-7 (sc)
ISBN: 978-1-4918-8432-4 (e)

CONTENTS

ACKNOWLEDGEMENTS

I would like to take this opportunity to thank all those people (well over 800 over the last five years) who have been on my:

- Job Club
- Work Club
- Business Club
- Fast Track to Success for Professionals/ Executives
- Fast Track to Success for Graduates
- Rock Star Mentees - Entrepreneurship

In particular, thanks should go to my Team of Mentors, Guest Speakers and Trainers who have supported these programmes – for further information please view www.ccoworkcic.com and www.workbizacademy.co.uk

This **'Fast Track to Success' Program** has over 50 Units and is based on the Institute of Leadership and Management, of which I am a Fellow, to deliver to Level 7. These Units are now available as E-Learning Packages through www.ccoworkcic.com. These

Units are now designed and produced according to Harvard Business School USA.

I have used the BELBIN Guide to How to Succeed at Work as a bible for this programme.

Other credits for support me with this book are:

'*The Rules of Work*' by Richard Templar, who kindly mentored me to prepare me for this book.

'*Screw It, Let's Do It* 'expanded by Richard Branson - who I have never had the pleasure of meeting, but I have previously worked for his Virgin Travel Group as a Consultant.

'*I'll Show Them Who's Boss*' by Gerry Robinson - Six Secrets of Successful Management. I have learnt not to put a Strategy to every Action and feel I have become a better Manager.

'*Marketing*' by Phil Harris, Dean of Entrepreneurship, University of Chester. I have had some enlightening and amusing conversations with Phil and greatly respect him.

Lord Sugar - Charlie Burden. I have not had the pleasure of working with Lord Sugar but when I moved from London to the North West 10 years ago he did respond to a request to introduce me to a CEO of a large corporation in St Helens - so I am grateful for that. Maybe I will end up on The Apprentice –I could certainly give them a run for their money!

'*The Warren Buffett Way* 'by Warren Buffett - such an incredible, amazing man and so humble.

INTRODUCTION

Of course, I learn from creating and writing all my own 'bespoke' programmes and then taking the learning journey with my clients - listening to employers and looking at my outcomes and taking note of my Appraisals to see how to improve to make sure that I give all our clients the 'edge' over contenders in a job interview. More importantly, I have a great team of Mentors and my programmes would not be the success they are without them. I listen to what they note on the journey whilst supporting people into employment. I run regular Yearly Training for my Mentors and we invite some past clients back to join us to become Mentors and give us feedback on how we can make the Programs even better. We then have a lovely lunch to celebrate our success which is sponsored by David Mowat MP for Warrington South, who is the Facilitator of our Work and Business Clubs in Warrington.

We are not even half way through 2013 and I have noted that for Graduate Programmes re: Employability they need to have more Social Media Workshops and Communication Skills. For my Professionals, it is Interview Techniques re: Assessments - Competency Based Q/A and lots more practice Interviews.

Success Rate

I have maintained an 86% success rate of achievement over the last five years for those who have attended my Programmes and are now in employment.

Purpose

My purpose for 2013 is to 'Learn – Live and Love' and boy …. I am certainly doing just that!

If you follow the process of this book, you will find the success you deserve.

I was viciously attacked in 2013 in Italy and I have not allowed this to hold me back - I believe in turning all negatives into POSITIVES and as one of my Mentors - Kal informed me, 'THAT I AM NOT A SURVIVOR BUT A THRIEVER!' At his suggested from attending some Workshops in London he gave me the book, 'The Law of DIVINE Compensation' by Marianne Williamson, which I read whilst I took myself of to Soul Weekend at Llandudno in July 2013 - where I danced the night away and then to continue the feeling of being free and in charge of my own destiny, walked home along the beach in the rain, that feeling of fresh, fine rain refreshing me left me in no doubt at all - that I am truly a THRIEVER! You can be also.

I am going to leave you with a quote from the above book, 'One of the most common negative self-concepts we carry - one that underlies many other wrong minded sentiments - is that we're simply not good enough; that something about us is defective.'

From the words of Confucious, 'Choose a job you love, and you will never have to work a day in your life.'

FOREWORD

'GET BRITAINWORKING'

As the Conservative Party moved forward with their above campaign, our local Conservative Party candidate for Warrington South, David Mowat MP, felt that it was the party's duty to tackle this problem locally with the increasing number of unemployed on the rise, particularly in the Executive/Graduate and even the 50 + groups where there was little support. I knew David through our charity work supporting young people and he asked me to write a programme to reflect supporting these Groups.

I had delivered **Executive/Job Clubs** in the last recession in London and **Graduate Programmes** working in partnership with DWP/JCP, Bethnal Green City Challenge and local councils, all working in partnership with the top London FTSE corporate companies from Price Waterhouse to Slaughter and May to Kleinwort Benson, supported by Paul Boateng MP, as he was then.

I then set about using a 'trend analysis'- a programme which reflected our new economic climate. This bespoke Programme is the basis for this book – **'Get Britain Working'**. I have to say that I changed the programme weekly as it was 'user led' and it had to reflect what the clients wanted and needed in terms of skills to successfully compete in today's job market. Since first writing this book I have modified it to reflect changes within the job market.

With over 3 million unemployed it will become more and more difficult – though there is a 'cloud with a silver lining'!

Graduates

'Fast Track to Success for Graduates' was written by me and delivered at Hope University, Liverpool, in 2013.

Yes, we are in a recession and graduates face a 5.4% cut in graduate vacancies for 2009. You have to get in touch – up your game – and equip yourself with the latest 'tools' (your secret weapons), which can be found in this book -and grab those opportunities, whether it be in the public sector ore-marketing etc. (see Top 10 Jobs). Salaries will remain the same, around £25K – though you will still earn more than those without a degree -and in any other unemployment periods to follow you will still be ahead of your colleagues (for *Management and Graduate Ability Test*, see www.shl.com).

We aim to generate self-esteem, upgrade skills and maintain skills to aid the process of Job Searching:

We will 'enhance' each individual's social networking circle and give them the motivation, support and skills to make a difference to their present economic and social position to enable them to find employment.

60% of jobs are found this way, which we call the 'Hidden Job Market'. We aim to enhance this programme with Work Placements for 1 to 4 weeks per month with local Employers. We also aim to use its connections with local businesses to support Social Networking.

This Programme is designed to develop your Job Search Skills to give you the opportunity of securing Work Experience so that you can WOW prospective employers.

According to an AGR Survey of Blue Chip companies in 2008/09 the skills needed by graduates to secure employment are listed below and will be covered on our programme: We continued this Survey using Social Media LinkedIn Groups Careers for the past 3 years' and find that Employers still felt that these skills are needed and what they look at when employing Graduates. We also in 2013 part of a Survey working with Hope University whilst delivering their EMPLOYABILITY PROGRAM sent this survey out across Liverpool using Networks such as Liverpool Chamber of Commerce to see if Employers could add to these skills. Based upon that Survey for 2014 - our Employability Programs will have even more Social Media Digital Workshops and Soft Skills based around COMMUNICATION which seems to stand alone as a major area for development.

Commitment	Problem Solving	Drive
Commercial Awareness	Motivation	Entrepreneurial Awareness
Leadership	Enthusiasm	Work Experience
Team Work	Oral Communication	

Time Bank reported that 73% of employers would rather employ someone with previous work experience.

Career Advancement

Even though promotions will be fewer as companies may have to cut back on spending, for those out there who are ambitious, this is your time to shine and push yourself forward. This is a time to re-evaluate yourself and develop your personal effectiveness (see *Personal Effectiveness – Mentoring*). This is the time for you to check your skill set, qualifications, image, and other areas from your appraisal at work to see what your employers want and to give it to them.

Professionals/Executives

These programmes have been delivered within the Work Club at Warrington and Chester from 2009 until 2013.

I have seen an increasing number of **executives** on my programme from middle to senior management.

This gives you the opportunity to look at your transferable skills, have a change of career and 'follow that dream' of becoming your own boss, be a consultant or set up your own business (see *Setting up Your Own Business*). Having been a consultant myself, there will be times – possibly 3 months in one year - where you will not work – feast or famine – so save for a rainy day!

Been Made Redundant?

Do not take this personally – it is not you that has been made redundant, but the job which became redundant. You are not alone and it has happened to us all and there is not one family in the UK that has not been affected by someone being made redundant at some time. My husband was made redundant, so I have been implementing this strategy with him and it worked – he got a job – albeit not the one he wanted, but it is a fresh start and it reinstated his confidence and has given him the opportunity to re-evaluate his skills and look at a new career challenge.

Women Returning To Work

You may have brought up your children and now want to return to work; your partner may have lost their job; or maybe you are a single parent who has to return to work. This is a good time to return to work with flexible hours in Retail with such companies as ASDA, Tesco, Iceland and Morrison who are all currently recruiting. Remember to be prepared, with a professional CV to reflect your transferable skills acquired whilst off work and always try to highlight experience from the voluntary sector. You will also find that some companies like Tesco and most public sector companies have a family friendly scheme which is reflected through offering flexi days for taking children to the dentist etc. My brother finds this particularly helpful whilst working at Tesco as a Manager, and even for when he wanted time off to take his family to a family rugby match.

50+

Not the end of your career or the world but a whole new beginning! There are many organisations which support you're. PRIDE through to The Prince's Trust for people 50+ wanting to start their own business and now also The Lavender Project. Proof of this was evident in my first job club programme where more than 50% were 50+. I do not agree that this becomes a disability, nor should it be looked at as one, as you will feel you are starting out on a negative journey before you begin – it is just another hurdle in life to overcome. I can do it – so can you! I completely reinvented myself and have never looked back. You just have to make sure that you highlight and 'showcase' all the valuable experience and skills that you have acquired – so that you 'stand out' in a competitive market.

Disadvantaged Groups

I have, in my career, worked with all types of groups, including ex-offenders, towards employability and Business Start-Ups and even worked in 2011 with Winning Pitch in partnership with G4S with a pilot for this client group. In 2012 we supported NHS – Wellbeing programmes working with people with mental illness and even supported ADS – working with people who have had problems with alcohol and drug addiction. This led us to realise that on these programmes there was a considerable number of clients who came to us with mental health issues, ranging from clients having been made redundant which led to depression; to being without employment, leading to seeking escape through abuse of alcohol and drugs. We also found that we started to work with a number of clients who were ex-servicemen.

What this book will do for you, as the programme did for my clients, is:

1. Give you confidence
2. Give you the tools to acquire that job
3. Motivate you to strive to achieve a 'dream job'.

I want you to sit back and enjoy the journey that this book will take you on, to a new level of self-confidence – are you ready to start to feeling good about yourself? Then read on!

Once you have read through this book you will have the tools to:

- Create that impressive CV
- Use Social Media to job search
- Attend network meetings
- Write business letters – Speculative Approach
- Make Application Forms work for you
- Improve your Interview Techniques
- Draw up your Action Plan
- Identify your strengths and weaknesses (areas for improvement)
- Psychometric Tests
- Recognise your Transferable Skills
- Develop a Marketing Strategy
- Develop an Employment Strategy
- Create your Personal Career Development Plan
- Improve your Leadership and Management skills
- Explore an Entrepreneurial Mindset.

TESTIMONIALS

CLIENTS

… "*Just to let you know I have been given a job working for E P Marketing Ltd. I will be starting on Monday morning. I'll speak to you more about it on Saturday. Again thank you so much for the support & advice you have given me so far, I hope that I will be able to continue the rest of the course over the coming weeks.*" **Phil Davies**

… "*I'm very grateful to have linked up with Chris Welsby from EP Printing under the excellent mentorship scheme. He is very approachable and understanding and I'm looking forward to his and his colleagues help, guidance and advice. He has a great sense of humour and seems to run a very interesting, innovative, bright and happy firm. I was very impressed with the enthusiasm, dedication and commitment shown by the accountant that broke the "boring accountant mould".1st class presentation - shame he didn't have a full audience. I thought he sold the idea of social media networking tremendously well. I will send him a personal email.*" **Malcolm**(thanks Malcolm! Ed.)

... *"Thank you very much for your detailed feedback, this is very positive. I really have never had anyone review my CV so this is an extremely useful exercise, Karen. I will revise...and yes, it is great having Louise as a mentor."* **Susan**

... *"Again, thanks to David (for setting the job club up), to you for your energy and experience and to Sheila for mentoring me at short notice."* **Neil**

... *"Many thanks for the encouraging feedback. Ironically, I didn't get a response to this job application, let alone an interview, but my CV was weak at this point and didn't reflect my capabilities as you rightly pointed out. My self confidence has always been my issue - this is why I've not achieved as high as I should have done on the career ladder. But I am feeling more inspired and encouraged from the programme and my mentor. Thank you."* **Susan**

... *"Wow! That's quite a lift on a Monday morning You truly are a woman of many talents, and we all should feel privileged to have met you and benefit from this experience. I was reflecting to her why I wanted to join the job club so much, it was that I heard a lot about you and instantly knew you were the right person to help me - God only knows how - but instinct I guess. You get things done - a woman after my own heart! Thanks again, I am humbled in your presence, and touched by your care, Blessings"* **Ruth.**

... *"Thanks for giving me those pointers. I do know that I have to start planning this career change. The* other thing is that I truly believe that in 12 months time I will also have a better job than the one which I left in May 2011 and that it will be entirely due to the toolset that have been demonstrated in the Job Club. I also think that they are absolutely suited to all levels - you just have to pick what suits - in my case I am taking everything on board. I feel incredibly lucky to have been able to attend this course for no cost." **Sonia**

… "I got the job as Assistant Manager at the gym in Gloucester on the quays and start next week on pre sale. We open 19th Dec, so looking forward to getting stuck in and being part of the management team back in the company again. I would like to say a big thank-you for all your help and advice- it has been a real breath of fresh air to meet you, you're ace!!Many thanks again Karen." **Jane :-) :-)**

… "I just wanted to thank you for all that you do for our group. The interview with David today gave me a real boost - I have only had about 3 interviews for jobs in the last 25 years! My problem has always been that I never get to the interview stage, but then you start wondering if you did, how would you get on. Anyway today I feel that I could handle any interview, which is what I thought really, but today confirmed my thoughts. I saw my mentor, Mustapha, this week too, and between him and David I now feel ready to move on with my business coaching ideas as I have more clarity about where I want to go with that. If you recall I said I wanted to start life coaching again to get moving but that I planned *to move on then to work more with businesses as that is where my heart lies. My USP is "To Improve the Customer Journey" which I am developing my thoughts on now. It was great to see people today looking dressed up and confident wasn't it? We have all come so far with your help and guidance and I was just thinking as I sat there today how wonderful it is that you are such a generous person, and how you pull so many people together to help those who are a bit down on their luck in the job stakes. It is difficult to see very far into the future when your confidence is low but I really feel that your programme helps people see that there are so many others in the same position as them, and others who have been there but are now back on their feet, which gives everyone hope. And we all need hope don't we? So, I'm sure you already know this but I would be happy to stay involved with you and help out as a mentor on your future programmes. I'm delighted how my two mentees are doing this time round and I can see both going on to great things by achieving their dreams. The name I came up with for my life coaching is "Find Your Dream" and working with these two along with my own situation is what brought me to this name. Anyway I'll let you go now but thank you for all your hard work - I want you to know it is appreciated, and I'll see you on Wednesday in Liverpool."* **Louise**

... *"Hope you remember me from the Saturday morning Job Club over in Stockton Heath wow, a couple of years ago now !!Just to jog your memory*

I was the ex Banker, Public House Manager and ex Director of a Transport Company who had a million ideas running through his head to earn his future millions and was really unable to make any of them stick! Sounds a very sad but true summary. Also hope you remember my attempts to sell you the benefits of my glossy flyer style CV....well I liked it. Even sadder, I fell into the trap that a lot of 50 is aged people fall into, drugs and alcohol. No seriously, when you're stuck as I got at 50 with rising debts it's the B&Q or Tesco/Morrison's/Asda route. I took the latter and for the past 2 years or so have worked at Asda on their Home Shopping Department where because of my experience I am a greatly valuable member of their team, even if I say so myself. I am not interested in going up the Managerial ladder with them as the pay is appalling and as a humble driver putting lots of hours in I can match the initial pay of a Departmental Manager who will have to do more hours than a driver to justify his salary. However,have had a business idea bubbling under for some time now and need to progress it further as I am very passionate that I can make a go of it this time. The good part about it is that I can initially work it in alongside my Asda work and as it takes off gradually drop Asda hours. So the pressure isn't really on the new business to kick in with a living income immediately which is where a lot of new businesses go wrong I feel. I enjoyed the benefit of your professional help and,indeed,the wonderful people that came along as mentors, course attendees and so on. My cheeky question to you now being is that sort of free help still available and

if so, being cheeky again, could I tap into it? I look forward to hearing from you and,Karen,without sounding patronizing it's been very useful for me to just have your contact details and be able to put my thoughts to you as a member of the 'real' business world rather than the world of Asda,if that makes sense. Look forward to hearing from you,
Regards" **Andy A**

... "I've written this recommendation of your work to share with other LinkedIn users. Details of the Recommendation: "Since first meeting Karen in September I believe she has totally turned my life around with her positive,dynamic,creative,well structured and expertly delivered programme; it's a shame 'we' have not got the technology to clone her. Her team of mentors and guest speakers are of an excellent quality and hopefully I have made some wonderful new associates and friends that I can call upon in the future. I feel totally empowered and looking forward to taking on the world again with my new business venture." **Service Category: Business Consultant**
Year first hired: 2012
Top Qualities: Personable, Expert, Creative

... "Will be in touch when I have received my letter. Thanks for all your help. Although the outcome was 'simple' through LinkedIn in the end - I have gained so much confidence and a new found self-being and worth through the work club." **Pat**

ENTERPRISE CLUB2012-11-30

... *"Thank you also Karen for your encouragement and support - I wouldn't have been so inspired without your help. You really work hard at this and in the end it's up to everyone else to get the job or start their business. You've done well. I feel I'm on top of everything and confident to really make a go of this. I will definitely make contact with those areas you have suggested and Ladies Forward. And I will keep in touch with how I'm progressing."* Add credit

GRADUATE TESTIMONIALS - 2013

... *"I attended a Fast Track Graduate Training Programme that was run by Karen over a two-day period. The programme provided me with an excellent insight as to how to successfully secure a career in the current economic climate. The use of social media in searching the hidden job market was extremely valuable; something that previous career advisors have failed to suggest. I also found the coverage of interview techniques to be useful, as this is undoubtedly a fundamental area in securing a career. This topic was warmly received by the group and enabled us to build confidence in an area that had previously been viewed as being daunting. I would strongly recommend Karen and the WorkBiz Academy to anyone wishing to gain a clear understanding of how to effectively search for a career."* **John Andrew Sellors - Hope University 2013**

... "Rob Woodhouse has recommended your work as Director at CcoworkCic.Com

... "I've written this recommendation of your work to share with other LinkedIn users.Details of the Recommendation: "I recently attended Karen's 'Bespoke Fast Track to Success Programme for Graduates', which I found to be extremely valuable and insightful. I am confident that this will be of significant benefit to me securing not just any job; but a job that I want and which will progress my career. Central to the value of the programme is Karen; her enthusiasm is contagious and she delivered the programme exceptionally, sharing many insights from her own experiences. Karen has a genuine desire to help, spending time to get to know everyone participating, and generously offered to appraise our CV's over the weekend. I have already started and will continue to implement the programme material to make my job hunt more focused and efficient. I would highly recommend this course to ALL graduates!"

... "Thank you so much for a brilliant course, although I know it was a highly condensed version of what you offer, I felt that I absorbed a lot of handy tips I hope to put to good use. I apologise again for leaving early, I was disappointed to miss the interview segment, do you have any PowerPoint slides or information sheets you could send me on interview techniques please? The reason I had to go was to attend an appointment at the job centre after having my hours cut at work where I support *learners on an employability course- the irony was painful. I am attaching a copy of my CV for you to give the once over, I appreciate you taking the time to do this for us. Hopefully it won't need too much tweaking, my Dad designed it for me (perhaps I should put delegation in my list of skills!)Best of luck in all your future endeavours,* **"Rebecca Jansen**

UNIT 1: USING MENTORING AS A TOOL TO SUPPORT YOU IN YOUR JOB SEARCH

Mentoring: What is Mentoring?

It comes from Greek Mythology.

I am a qualified and well experienced Mentor with over 20 years' experience through the Institute of Leadership & Management (ILM)including as a Business Mentor at UCLAN (University of Central Lancashire, Preston) on their Northern Lights Programme; Business Start Programmes for PERA/ BIS; Winning Pitch; Rockstar Group and many more....

Mentors

The success of my programmes is contributed to the value and experience of my Mentors, whose passion and support has driven this success. Without their contribution, these programmes would not have achieved the phenomenal outcomes that we have had.

During the Induction, the Mentors introduce themselves and there is advantage of choosing your very own Mentor to enable you to achieve success.

I tend to use the SIROLLI Method: This enables **Enterprise** to move forward. I used this method of Mentoring for each client offering them the opportunity of having a Mentor in their chosen career. Alternatively, some chose a Mentor that they identified would support their new business or business growth.

Personal Effectiveness

Using a two pronged approach, this method was used to develop, individually, the client's communication skills through personal development.

What is Mentoring?

It is to encourage and support our clients to develop their own individual development through a journey from being unemployed to being 'back in the game' and considered for employment and thus securing employment. We concentrate on maximising their potential and showcasing their skills, improving their performance and leading them onto becoming the person they want to be.

It gives EMPOWERMENT to people for them to progress and is an effective tool and this becomes a CONTRACT between two people to fulfil the client's potential, based upon trust between the Mentor and the Mentee. I feel it does help if the Mentor has shared similar experiences which they can draw upon and I certainly use this as an 'edge' in my mentoring.

The Mentor ....

.... must gain empathy, trust and respect with the Mentee and be understanding of the Mentee's position. The Mentor should boost the confidence of the Mentee and install the feeling of 'self belief', as well as demonstrating strategies to explore and encourage new ideas. Everything must be done in the strictest confidence.

The Mentee ...

... has the opportunity to explore new ideas; to look more closely at themselves and explore those hidden aspirations; to become more self aware and take the responsibility for their actions –to self promote in order to deliver and achieve. It is their chance to 'take control'!

Mentoring:

- Is completed in the strictest confidence
- Establishes a set of boundaries/rules
- Involves limited paperwork
- Offers flexibility
- Motivates

- Inspires

- Challenges

- Ensures that the Mentee takes control, makes decisions and takes action.

A typical session should consist of:

- An introduction to the partnership between the Mentor and the Mentee to establish rapport;

- The Mentee then states their ground/ case;

- They agree the areas to be discussed;

- At the end of the session the Mentor agrees an Action Plan with the Mentee for the next session;

- The Mentor makes recommendations with the Mentee's agreement and the Mentor records their comments.

This form is then signed by both as a Contract and a date is agreed to meet again.

Note: There are various ways of Mentoring – face to face, group work, telephone, email or text – Mentors should indicate which in each session.

The Mentor will keep up regular contact with the Mentee before the next meeting by whatever method both have agreed. I prefer emailing and see this as a way of e-learning.

Once you have got over the first session, the rest just flows. I find, though, that if you arrive at a session and the Mentee has not action the agreed Plan then the Mentee has not honoured their side of the contract and you would have to consider whether you have established rapport or empathy.

I have never had this happen to me and I have avoided this by contacting the Mentee before the session by email, followed up by a call to establish boundaries and advise what will be expected of the Mentee. At any time, either party can decide whether or not to continue with the Partnership.

To bring this Partnership to conclusion, I allow the Mentee to draw a line under the contract and let them state that they no longer need the Mentor and that they have achieved what was agreed in their Action Plan.

UNIT 2: GROUP DYNAMICS – TEAMWORK

After an Introduction from me and my Mentors we have to learn to work as a Group and we centre some Ice Breakers around Group Dynamics / Team Work. In the world of work, this is what employers are looking for.

EXCERCISE ONE

Introduce yourself – take 3 minutes: Who are you – what do you do and what do you want to achieve?

EXERCISE TWO

Now working in pairs: You have 3 minutes to find out as much as possible about the other person and then give a 90second Presentation to the Group.

UNIT 3: STRENGTHS AND WEAKNESSES

We, as a team, need to indentify strengths and weaknesses to deliver successful outcomes. This exercise will support you to identify the above and use these in your CV – Profiles – LinkedIn – Social Media and Interview Techniques.

Write down a list of 12 of each.

STRENGTHS

FUNCTIONAL SKILLS: are what you can do re: a skill base – ICT Skills for example.

CORE SKILLS: are what you have as personal attributes – Outstanding organisational skills for example.

WEAKNESSES

You will learn in this programme to work on your weaknesses and turn these into strengths.

For example: If your weakness is ICT Skills – then state that you are updating these using on line e-learning and state that in previous employment you had volunteered for internal training, are willing in your own time and with your own funds to support further development.

UNIT 4: PERSONALITY TYPES

Strengths and Weaknesses of the Types – Personality

Now that you have valued your strengths and know your weaknesses - using the principles of BELBIN here are some of the roles that you would play within a Team.

Who are you?

Are you several Roles?

ROLES: Please see below and decided what you are and that of your Team.

A Summary of the Belbin Team Role model		
Team Role	**Strengths**	**Weaknesses**
Shaper	Challenging, dynamic, goal oriented, has drive and courage	Prone to provocation and can be blunt and upset people

Implementer	Disciplined, organised, efficient, turns ideas into actions	Somewhat inflexible, slow to embrace change or accept new ideas
Completer Finisher	Accurate, conscientious, meticulous perfectionist	Inclined to worry unduly, reluctant to delegate
Resource Investigator	Enthusiastic, communicative, explores opportunities, develops contacts	Over-optimistic, easily bored and can lose interest
Co-ordinator	Calm, confident, clarifies goals, promotes joint decision making	Can be seen as manipulative, off-loads personal work
Team worker	Cooperative, caring, diplomatic, sensitive, averts friction	May be indecisive when faced with tough decisions
Plant	Creative, imaginative, original, offers alternative approaches	Pre-occupied by thoughts and may not be communicative

Monitor Evaluator	Logical, analytical, discerning, makes decisions based on facts	Appears slow moving, lacks drive and may appear uninspiring
Specialist	Single minded, motivated by the pursuit of knowledge	Contributes on a narrow front, dwells on technicalities

UNIT 5: VOLUNTARY WORK–ENHANCING YOUR OPPORTUNITIES OF EMPLOYMENT

Volunteering –What's in it for you?

People take part in Volunteering for various reasons and on this Programme you should engage in up to 16 hours of Volunteering work per week in line with JCP guidelines re your benefits to:

- Gain valuable work experience in a certain field or new field

- Meet new people – social networking

- Develop existing skills or learn new ones

- Enjoy a sense of personal achievement

- Have something positive to put onto your CV

- Make use of any spare time

- Have a strong affinity to a certain cause and want to make a difference

- Work as part of a team and have lots of fun and enjoyment.

Volunteering will give you a great deal of satisfaction in the knowledge that you are really making that difference.

There are various opportunities available and you can choose an area of interest: see your local www. cvs.org.uk or www.info@vc.org.uk

For example, if you have IT skills and your interest is to work in Mental Health, then contact Mental Health Forums for a list of organisations in your area. Some of your local authorities will have a database of the voluntary organisations listed with vacancies, or contact your local CVS centre.

UNIT 6: CV PREPARATION

This is an introduction to creating that CV which will do you proud!

CV comes from the Latin meaning Course for Life and highlights your skills/experience.

Using my format, which I have used with Morgan Hunt Recruiters and which has done me proud for the last 5 years and secured 4 out of 5 interview opportunities for me, please pay attention to the:

- Style and presentation
- Use 8 sections; put headings in **bold** and aim to put the information onto two pages.
- Spelling and grammar. It is imperative to get someone to proof read **before** you send it off and make use of your spell check – any CV sent with mistakes in either spelling or grammar is usually binned.

Your CV is your passport to success and to securing that interview - then you are on your way!

Remember that competition is fierce and in the current economic climate jobs are fewer and fewer. You need to make sure that your CV is not:

- Overlooked
- Passed by
- Fails to impress
- Binned.

I learnt from the Master of the CV – Max Eggert – 'The Perfect CV' and I still use the same format, except I now use Social Media to enhance the CV.

UNIT 7: GENERIC CV

This is a generic CV – you should tailor each CV for each area of work and slightly tweak it to suit the Job Description of each job.

Section 1– Name and address

This needs to be in full with a correct postal code. It has to include your telephone number/s both home and mobile, and your email address – then they should have no trouble in getting hold of you quickly to discuss an interview date!

NEW – add your LINKEDIN Profile – this is now where employers look for additional information and gives them a FULL profile of you.

Section 2 – Personal Profile

Please highlight:

- Skills and qualities
- Career aims
- Strengths will play into this.

In 6-10 lines - be specific to the job you are applying for – you can change this section to highlight the job description each time.

Example:

If it is to work with people, say you are an exceptional team player and an effective communicator and keep it brief.

Section 3 – Key Skills

Use bullet points, be positive and clearly label your most up-to-date skills to secure the job you want.6-10 points would be fine.

Example:

If you have experience in fundraising, state what type, for example was it SRB, ESF,ERDF, corporate etc. – anything that is specific to your area.

Section 4 – Significant Achievements

List two to four things you have achieved in your work/community life related to your work history and job.

Example:

If you want to work for a Charity or in the Third Sector

- You organised the Warrington Homeless Christmas Ball in partnership with Warrington Wolves in 2007.

Section 5 – Employment History

Always in reverse order with your last job first – going back 10 years. NB: Please double check when completing an application form, as very occasionally they want the order to be by year starting with when you left school/college/university.

Example:

Dates to and from	Establishment/ Company	Title/Job description

Section 6 – Education & Training – Voluntary Work can be added here

In reverse order with most recent first.

Example:

Dates	Establishment	Subject/Qualification	Grade

Include in the above any additional WORK RELATED TRAINING or COURSES, whether internal or external.

Example:

First Aid Training, ECDL Training

Section 7 – Hobbies and Interests

These are Personal but don't list too many as this could indicate you would not have time for your work. Have a good balance and highlight some family activities, community, social, sports and relaxation.

Never lie about this as you could get someone interviewing you who is an avid reader of crime and that is what you stated – be honest and factual!

Section 8 – References

I always put 'supplied on request' because you may not want your Referees being contacted all the time – only when you have *that job*!

In preparation, you can create a separate page TODAY with:

Four references; two work related and two character giving;

- Name
- Address
- Contact number/s
- E mail addresses.

If it is an employer, then submit their full title. Try to influence and be ahead of your competition; use people high up within the company but who know your capabilities.

For a character reference, use people within the community that are impressive but only if they have known you personally for more than three years – MPs, Councillors etc.

Now you are ready to produce that masterpiece – your Passport for success.

NOTE:

Using your phone you can load up your CV to www.cvbrowser.com ready to send to prospective employers.

UNIT 8: TECHNICAL CV

Dewy Roland Williams
Address
Postcode
Tel number

A highly professional Quality Manager with specific expertise in quality assurance, product safety and evaluating and testing consumer products. Possesses extensive experience in establishing and managing effective quality systems, and UKAS accreditation as well as interpreting legislation, standards and technical documentation.

Career History

2007 – 2009   Ultimate Products Ltd – Importers of consumer goods for retailers and Supermarkets – Senior Quality Assurance Technologist

- Formally documented product requirements allowing the buying team a formal product benchmark, thereby substantially reducing product development time and improving customer service.

- Documented product defect classification lists for use by shipment inspectors to a common standard thus enabling them to be interpreted more easily and ensuring consistency.

- Presented in-house training to colleagues on QA issues and procedures.

- Dramatically reduced both costs and time spent testing electrical products for RoHS compliance by the introduction of a portable XRF Analyser for in-house testing.

- Developed product expertise in furniture, memory foam products, toys and home wares including ceramics, cutlery and cookware.

- Evaluated new products for quality as well as compliance with legal requirements such as the General Product Safety Directive, RoHS, REACH, Packaging Waste Regulations as well as product specific requirements.

2007 – 2007 RMS International Importers and Distributors of Consumer Goods Quality Assurance Manager – 4 month contract.

- Successfully managed a UKAS surveillance visit resulting in renewal of laboratory UKAS accreditation.

2005 – 2006 Bureau Veritas Consumer Product Services
Hardliners Manager

- Substantially reduced overdue jobs from 56% of work in progress to 91.5%, which also improved customer service.

- Negotiated project specifications and commercial terms with clients.

- Developed a new business activity for the company by researching and pioneering a series of tests which satisfied the BSI and the Road Traffic Act in terms of newly introduced standards for bicycle safety.

- Enhanced the company's reputation as a source of expert advice which helped to generate business in a new product area.

1990 – 2005 RMS International
Quality Assurance Manager

- Established the company laboratory and QA department for product evaluation and certification leading to:

    a) Significant reduction in turn-around time and testing costs compared to using 3rd party laboratories.

    b) Faster and more effective resolution of complaints from both customers and Trading Standards.

c) Improvement in the company's reputation as a responsible supplier with both customers and Trading Standards Officers from various Local Authorities.

- Documented the laboratory quality manual and associated procedures leading to a successful application for UKAS accreditation.

- Maintained the laboratory quality system including document control, internal and external audits and quality checks, equipment calibration and surveillance visits by UKAS auditors.

- Developed and implemented new test methods based on product standards and updated methods and procedures in line with changes in standards and legislation.

- Monitored standards, legislation and EC Directives and advised the company on how they applied to the product range.

- Successfully developed in-house expertise to assist the buying team in product development and resolving customer queries.

1989 – 1990   Astor Chemical
Research and Development Chemist

1989 – 1989   Conoco
Shift Chemist

Professional Qualifications
Member of Royal Society of Chemistry
Member of the Institute of Quality Assurance
IQA Quality Assurance Management Qualification
– University of Salford
BScHons Applied Chemistry – Nottingham Trent
University

Training
Courtroom Skills Course – Bond Solon
Auditing in UKAS laboratories – ERA Technology
Safety Development Certificate – ROSPA

Interests

- Chief Safety Officer for firework display
  at annual School PTA event

- Chief Marshall at Appleton Thorn
  Bawming Day

- TVR Owners club member

- Maintaining physical fitness through
  cycling and visiting the gym.

UNIT 9: GRADUATE CV

Photo   **NAME**
Headshot if required   **ADDRESS**
                          TEL NOS
                          EMAIL ADDRESS
                          LinkedIn link

PERSONAL PROFILE

I am a recent BA Honours 2.1 Graduate in English with a desire and passion to work in the Media Industry. To compliment this achievement I have gained 3 years' significant experience working at MEN Media in a variety of roles whilst studying. I am articulate and presentable with a flair for communication on all levels.

SCHOLARSHIPS AND AWARDS

QUALIFICATIONS

SKILLS

- ICT SKILLS – Excel – Word

SIGNIFICANT ACHIEVEMENTS

- Chair of the Liverpool Hope University Debating Society 2010- 2013

EMPLOYMENT DETAILS (include VOLUNTARY ROLES) reverse Date Order date

Dates/to/from   Company   Title   Duties

EDUCATION/TRAINING – Reverse Date Order

Dates/to/from   Establishment   Qualification   Result

LEISURE INTERESTS

References supplied on request

THE PERFECT GRADUATE CV

↘ROB WOODHOUSE

Frodsham, Cheshire | Willing to relocate
m. 07868848015 t. 01928 734681
woodhouse.rob@gmail.com
uk.linkedin.com/in/robwoodhouse1/

↘PERSONAL PROFILE

I am a recent MSc Psychology graduate actively seeking an Assistant Psychologist role. To complement this achievement I have experience of working with children with ASD, and experience of drafting articles for publication. My varied background has equipped me with numerous transferable skills including problem solving, as well as communication and research skills.

↘ SCHOLARSHIPS &aWARDS

- Represented University by presenting dissertation research as a poster at a Conference at Hope University in incorporating feedback into subsequent research.

- Co-authored an article which is currently undergoing peer review for the Journal of Cognitive Psychology

- Member of the University Psychology Ethics Committee, demonstrating intergroup communication, analysis and increased knowledge base of experimental design.

- Elected by peers to be student/staff liaison for MSc Psychology.

⅏ QUALIFICATIONS

MSc Psychology, Distinction, Liverpool Hope University (2013) - Graduate Member of BPS

⅏ SKILLS

Analytical Thinking	Resolve problems using a logical yet creative approach
ICT	Microsoft Office, including Word, PowerPoint, Excel; SPSS
Communication	Oral and written, demonstrated through the production of company literature and the delivery of presentations
Adaptability	Adapt to changing job demands quickly and effectively
Research	Conducted comprehensive literature review and proven experience of quantitative and a knowledge of qualitative research
Commitment	Motivated and committed to all projects undertaken with high expectations for my contribution and success

⬎ SIGNIFICANT ACHEIVEMENTS

- Analysed and implemented efficiency measures at Woodhouse Ltd, increasing profitability;

- Implemented office processes, allowing more productive use of employee time;

- Drafted and secured approval for a broad range of policy and operational documentation for Woodhouse Ltd, working in collaboration with colleagues and external consultants;

- Re-branded and produced company marketing literature, advertising and vehicle decals.

⬎ EMPLOYMENT DETAILS

07/2012 - 02/2013   Office / Operations Manager
Woodhouse Plumbing, Heating & Electrical Ltd.

- Acquired commercial experience through a central role within a small but growing business. Central to this role was financial management, budgeting and cash flow analysis. Organised ongoing projects and operations, further developed marketing and advertising strategy, and researched areas for business growth. Written and oral communication skills were progressed through production of reports, the development of an operations manual and the delivery of company presentations. Where possible psychological knowledge was used to improve and implement procedures.

01/2012 - 05/2012 ASD Assistant
ASD Unit, Middlewich High School - Volunteer Post (1 day per week).

- Provided support and assistance to ASD children to be more effective learners.

03/2011 - 07/2012   Projects Assistant
        S Downs Building Ltd.

09/2010 - 03/2011   Site Assistant
        Oakwood Homes Construction Ltd.

04/2004 - 09/2010   Waiter
        Forest Hills Hotel

⬎ EDUCATION / TRAINING

2010-11	Open University	Discovering Psychology	60 Credits	Distinction
2007-10	Northumbria University	Architecture	BA	2:1
2004-06	Sir John Deanes' College	Psychology	A level	B
2004-06	Sir John Deanes' College	Chemistry	A level	C
2004-06	Sir John Deane's College	Biology	A level	D
1999-2004	Bishops' High School	6 (inc. English & Maths)	GCSE	A-B
1999-2004	Bishops' High School	ICT	GNVQ	Merit

⬎ LEISURE INTERESTS

I have a keen interest in current affairs, with particular consideration to human factors and motivations. Committed to fitness, I regularly run, circuit train and ski whenever possible. I enjoy socialising, be it at live music or comedy events. I am an avid reader of psychology, science and philosophy books. Being self motivated and ambitious on many levels, this comes across most notably in my commitment to a successful career through my desire to help others.

↘ REFERENCES

Available on request

UNIT 10: PROFESSIONAL/ EXECUTIVE CV

For those of you with only the last 3 years' personal/ professional development. You may for some industries use a Passport Photograph to be inserted on the top left hand corner. It is more common than ever for customer focused organisations.

Name
Address- include postcode
Contact numbers – try to include land line
E mail address
LinkedIn Link

Personal Profile
6 lines only of "what **I** do now, what **I'm** looking for and what **I** want to do".

Do not use the 3rd person!

Professional Education

Your personal development over the last 3 years

Key Skills

Evidence based on your last jobs over the previous 10 years

Significant Achievements

Minimum of three and preferably employment based

Employment

Influence, demonstrate your successes and skills, capabilities and potential

(in order with the most recent first)

Dates to and from   Organisation/Company
        Job title/Brief description -
        Name and Address   Significant achievement

Education/Training

(in order with the most recent first)

Dates to and from   Establishment/college   Course
                                      title/Grade/Pass
                                      Name and address

Leisure Interests

6 – 10 most recent hobbies/interests

For example:

Karen Melonie Gould
Cheshire
(079391 64110m)
karen@workbizacademy.co.uk**http://www.
linkedin.com/profile/view?id=162158936&trk=nav_
responsive_tab_profile**

PERSONAL PROFILE

An accomplished Strategic Business Development Executive, I am self-motivated, innovative and an inspirational, pro-active thinker, creating and delivering bespoke Programmes, Solutions and Workshops for SMEs, Professionals, Executives,working to strategic objectives to deliver/exceed outcomes. A true, robust ENTREPRENEUR who delivers with passion and with creative, innovative and charismatic flair. Outstanding business accruement with a robust approach using Lean/ILM Principles using my International Operational Expertise and Project Management Leadership skills and expertise to deliver change.

PROFESSIONAL EDUCATION/TRAINING

Sep 2011	CMI	Business Mentoring and Coaching 5
July 2010	ILM	Fellow – Level 7
Sep 2009	University of Chester	MBA Business Administration
Jan 2009	MMC	PMS Project Management

KEY SKILLS

- Business Start Ups/ Development – Advisor/ Mentor/Trainer
- Commissioning bids/tenders/Access to Finance SMEs
- Public Sector Contracts with BIS/JCP – NAVCA/ SEN/Councils
- Effective and highly motivated Guest Speaker/ Author and Trainer
- Strategic Change/Culture Project Management – Lean/Fellow ILM/PMS
- Outstanding interpersonal/communication skills – Social Networking/Events
- Management of teams re: Training & Development of up to 400 personnel
- Accomplished business acumen - set-up and developed SME companies
- Organisational flair and co-ordination expertise – Corporate Events/PR
- Assessing/Monitoring/Evaluating/PM skills – DASHBOARD/SAP/ICT
- Research and Development re Innovation/ Academia/Corporate/Enterprise.

SIGNIFICANT ACHIEVEMENTS

- UK Women's Enterprise Ambassador 2012
- Board Member of LEP – Employer Skills/Enterprise/ Business Cheshire
- Nominated by Lord Wei for 'Big Society' Award - 2011

- Runner Up, Cheshire Woman of the Year 2011/ WBV Business Woman
- Author of self help books 2013 - *'Fast Track to Success'*
- Business Angel NW.

EMPLOYMENT HISTORY

Jan 2012 - Present - Business Mentor and Speaker, Rockstar Group/Lead Partner NW/NE Start Up Loans Rockstar Youth - Mentoring - Workshops and Partnership collaboration. Also delivering Entrepreneurship Workshops.

Jan 2012 – Created WorkBiz Academy to deliver Master Classes in Professional/Executive Career Search – Business Start Up and Development.

Jan 2009 – Present – CCO WORK CIC/WorkBiz Academy – Director – Currently delivering Fast Track to Success Employability Programs Academia.

2010/2011 for Warrington and Cheshire. Over 50+ JCP Programme Mentor/Trainer. Sales Director Careerplan4me for NW.BCT Regenesis/Bank of America/NWDA – Business Mentor.SEN – Business Mentor.

2009- Present - Wrote and Delivered Work/Job Club and Business Enterprise Club for David Mowat MP, Conservative Party, Warrington. 76% success rate

Nov 08 – April 09 - Manchester City Council, Project Manager/Commissioner - 26 Projects/£4M budget/created the Commissioning Model for Children/Youth Services.

Oct 07 – Present   UCLAN – Northern Lights Programme – SME/Development Mentor – OUTSTANDING OFSTED/ SFEDI UK Runner Up

Mar 07 – May 08   YMCA/Warrington – Business/ Fundraising Development & Training Manager – Raised £25k Charity Homeless Event

Apr 06 –Mar 07   Manchester City Council - Senior Communications Officer – Liaising and solving problems raised in Education

Mar 05 – Mar 06   SHWDA – Business/Training Development Manager – Raised over £750K FIRSTSTEPS Training Programme/delivered.

May 04 – Feb 05   Liverpool Vision – Regeneration Officer – Capital of Culture – Coordinating Events - City of Light and Japanese Visit

Sep 99 – Apr 04   Advanced Training/Gold Introductions – Director – Training and Business Development and a Social Networking Company created and built up companies to have £3.4m turnover in 5 yrs.

Oct 98 – Sep 99	Tower Hamlets Council – Training and Development Manager
Aug 90 – Sep 98	Hackney Council – Employment and Training Manager
Mar 85 – May 90	Airtours – Funjet Holidays – USA – Training/OP Director

LEISURE INTERESTS –

Zumba Instructor - Travel, Dancing, Fashion, Music, People, Socialising/Networking – Reading, Current Affairs and Life in General.

UNIT 11: CLOUD APPLICATION – DIGITAL CREATION OF CVS

USING WORD CLOUDS for CV

1. Free Online Programme: Log on to www.wordle.net

2. Open Create section

3. Open your CV in Microsoft Word

4. Copy CV content

5. Paste CV content into top box section on Create page - Paste in your selection of text

6. Press Go

7. Word Cloud in colour appears after a few seconds

8. Go to Layout and scroll to Horizontal (Optional)

9. Go to Colour and scroll to WB (White on Black I like, Optional)

10. Under Language, scroll to bottom to see Word Counts for more information on word frequency in document

11. Underneath the Word Cloud are options to Open in Window or Print (I use Print to save in PDF format)

12. The larger the word in the cloud, the more important it is in the document

13. Repeat process for any job description you are thinking of applying for

14. Compare the job description keywords with your CV keywords; modify your CV for applying for the job as required using new keyword phrases

15. Check revised CV through Wordle to see new fit prior to submitting CV

16. Key Tip: When looking at generic CV, process up to 9 interesting job descriptions through Wordle and pick most relevant to introduce into your CV.

TELEPHONE APP - download

www.cvbrowser.com - set this up on your phone and send your CV whilst on the go!

UNIT 12: PSYCHOMETRIC TESTS

Psychometric Testing – Selby & Mills and Koogan Page

The above have FREE Trials and you must practise these until you sail through

This is a phenomenon in the UK in recruiting. It is an integral part of the hiring process. It is due to the high cost of recruitment and helps the employer make the right choice.

These are **Personality Questionnaires** and you can improve your **Employability** by receiving **coaching** on this and of course – plenty of practice!

Companies are using these to:

- Select their right type of person i.e. Team Player
- Personality traits i.e. Team Player.

They use **Occupational Psychologists** to compile this information. Your answers are interpreted by Test Administrators in HR and they conclude **facts** about you based on your answers.

Strengths and Weaknesses (Areas for Development)

We are going to work as a Team to identify your Strengths and Weaknesses (areas for development) and will compare this from your online test and from your Appraisal at the end of this Programme to see if you have gained more strengths and now how fewer weaknesses.

Please log on to: www.selbymills.co.uk/ and for the next 20 minutes this will focus on:

Customer Service skills
People Management skills
Business Quality – Management skills
Professional skills

You can also purchase a *"Management Potential - 64 Questions"* at a cost of £14.95 and which will take you around 10 minutes to complete.

If you register with a reputable Agency in your field of work, though, they will complete these for you.

So, after this Introduction you will not be anxious about these again! Will you?

Conclusion

At the end of this Programme you will be able to rapidly answer the questions in the safe knowledge that your chances of employment remain intact.

You should not be job searching7 days a week as two days a week should be used to showcase your skills to make a difference – learning new skills, meeting new people and making new contacts is better than watching day time TV.

Get out there – they need your skills and you need their support, Good Luck!

Psychometric tests are widely used in all organisations now from ASDA to KMPG, from Marks & Spencer to NWDA.

It is a Report based on interpreting data supplied by you by answering multiple choice questions Your answers will provide the employer with a trend in your attitude.

An example would be the format used by ASDA/TESCO which is a small A5 booklet with several questions and given choices, reflecting whether you would fit into a team at one of their stores. It is not a Test – but does need honest answers reflecting team work.

Whilst at NWDA this came in the form of an on-line 45 minute multiple choice questionnaire. This, together with a CV/Application form, was used as a selection process for interview. Prior to the interview, a whole morning would be spent on various tests from IT, English and Maths before demonstrating your IT skills within a group situation relating to Team work – this was prior to your Presentation and Interview.

Selby & Mills is the most common form of this testing – see info@selbymills.co.uk – most now charge for this service which on average is around £25. You need to practise these as frequently as possible and employers do unfortunately spend considerable money and time evaluating this information – so you need to get it right.

This Test will produce evidence under various headings from 'STRIVING FORSUCCESS'to'THINKING AND ACTING AHEAD'.

Additional reading

Peter Honey – *Honey and Mumford Learning Styles* – www.peterhoney.com

For a learning styles Profiler with self–development feedback report –free – www.cymeon.com

Chris Jackson – Explores the effectiveness of the Jackson Hybrid Model of Learning in Personality.

Word of note

I used to be too analytical when attempting these and was really scared – now after much practise I have followed my learning journey with this and keep all past tests and note that I score well above average – so I am now confident in this task.

Personal Style Inventory
[© R. Craig Hogan and David W. Champagne][1]

The purpose of this inventory is to give you a picture of the shape of your preferences, but that shape, while different from the shapes of other person's personalities, has nothing to do with mental health or mental problems.

The following items are arranged in pairs ('a' and 'b') and each member of the pair represents a preference you may or may not hold. Rate your preference for each item, by giving it a score on a scale ranging from 0 to 5. (For example, 0 meaning you really feel negative about it or strongly about the other member of the pair, and 5 meaning you strongly prefer it or do not prefer the other member of the pair). The scores for 'a' and 'b' must add up to 5. For example: 0 and 5, or 1 and 4, or 2 and 3, etc.) Do not use fractions such as 2.5.

[1]   Copyright © 1979 by D. W. Champagne and R. C. Hogan. Reprinted with permission of the authors from the privately published book, *Supervisory and Management Skills: A competency-Based Training Program for Middle Managers of Educational Systems* by D. W. Champagne and R. C. Hogan. This material may be freely reproduced for educational/training/research activities. There is no requirement to obtain special permission for such uses. However, systematic or large-scale reproduction or distribution – or inclusion of items in publications for sale – may be done only with prior written permission of the authors.

I prefer:		Score
1.	a) Making decisions after finding out what others think.	
	b) Making decisions without consulting others.	
2.	a) Being called imaginative or intuitive.	
	b) Being called factual and accurate.	
3.	a) Making decisions about people in organisations based on available data and systematic analysis of situations.	
	b) Making decisions about people in organisations based on empathy, feelings, and understanding of their needs and values.	
4.	a) Allowing commitments to occur if others want to make them.	
	b) Pushing for definite commitments to ensure that they are made.	
5.	a) Quiet, thoughtful time alone.	
	b) Active, energetic time with people.	
6.	a) Using methods I know well that are effective to get the job done.	
	b) Trying to think of new methods of doing tasks when confronted with them.	

I prefer:		Score
7.	a) Drawing conclusions based on unemotional logic and careful step-by-step analysis.	
	b) Drawing conclusions based on what I feel and believe about life and people from past experiences.	
8.	a) Avoid making deadlines.	
	b) Seeking a schedule and sticking to it.	
9.	a) Talking a while and then thinking to myself about the subject.	
	b) Talking freely for an extended period and thinking to myself at a later time.	

10.	a)	Thinking about possibilities.
	b)	Dealing with actualities.
11.	a)	Being thought of as a thinking person.
	b)	Being thought of as a feeling person.
12.	a)	Considering every possible angle for a long time before and after making a decision.
	b)	Getting the information I need, considering it for a while, and then making a fairly quick, firm decision.
13.	a)	Inner thoughts and feelings others cannot see.
	b)	Activities and occurrences in which others join.
14.	a)	The abstract or theoretical.
	b)	The concrete or real.
15.	a)	Helping others explore their feelings.
	b)	Helping others make logical decisions.
16.	a)	Change and keeping options open.
	b)	Predictability and knowing in advance.
17.	a)	Communicating little of my inner thinking and feelings.
	b)	Communicating freely my inner thinking and feelings.
18.	a)	Possible views of the whole.
	b)	The factual details available.
19.	a)	Using common sense and conviction to make decisions.
	b)	Using data, analysis and reason to make decisions.
20.	a)	Planning ahead based on projections.
	b)	Planning as necessities arise, just before carrying out the plans.
21.	a)	Meeting new people.
	b)	Being alone, or with one person I know well.

22.	a)	Ideas.	
	b)	Facts.	
23.	a)	Convictions.	
	b)	Verifiable conclusions.	
24.	a)	Keeping appointments and notes about commitments in notebooks or in appointment books as much as possible.	
	b)	Using appointment books as little as possible (although I may use them).	
25.	a)	Discussing a new, unconsidered issue at length in a group.	
	b)	Puzzling out issues in my mind, then sharing the results with another person.	
26.	a)	Carrying out carefully laid, detailed plans with precision.	
	b)	Designing plans and structures without necessarily carrying them out.	
27.	a)	Logical people.	
	b)	Feeling people.	
28.	a)	Being free to do things on the spur of the moment.	
	b)	Knowing well in advance what I am expected to do.	
29.	a)	Being the centre of attention.	
	b)	Being reserved.	
30.	a)	Imagining the non-existent.	
	b)	Examining details of the actual.	
31.	a)	Experiencing emotional situations, discussions and motives.	
	b)	Using my ability to analyse situations.	
32.	a)	Starting meetings at a pre-arranged time.	
	b)	Starting meetings when all are comfortable or ready.	

Personal Style Inventory – Scoring Sheet Instructions

Transfer your scores for each item of each pair to the appropriate blanks. Be careful to check the 'a' and 'b' letters to be sure you are recording scores in the appropriate blank spaces. Then total the scores for each dimension.

Dimension I	Dimension E	Dimension N	Dimension S
Item	Item	Item	Item
1b. _____	1a. _____	2a. _____	2b. _____
5a. _____	5b. _____	6b. _____	6a. _____
9a. _____	9b. _____	10a. _____	10b. _____
13a. _____	13b. _____	14a. _____	14b. _____
17a. _____	17b. _____	18a. _____	18b. _____
21b. _____	21a. _____	22a. _____	22b. _____
25b. _____	25a. _____	26b. _____	26a. _____
29b. _____	29a. _____	30a. _____	30b. _____
Total I _____	Total E _____	Total N _____	Total S _____

Dimension T	Dimension F	Dimension P	Dimension J
Item	Item	Item	Item
3a. _____	3b. _____	4a. _____	4b. _____
7a. _____	7b. _____	8a. _____	8b. _____
11a. _____	11b. _____	12a. _____	12b. _____
15b. _____	15a. _____	16a. _____	116b. _____
19b. _____	19a. _____	20b. _____	20a. _____
23b. _____	23a. _____	24b. _____	24a. _____
27a. _____	27b. _____	28a. _____	28b. _____
31b. _____	31a. _____	32b. _____	32a. _____
Total T _____	Total F _____	Total P _____	Total J _____

Interpretation:

Key to the letters on the score sheet

Extraversion (E)

Prefers to draw energy from the outer world of activity, people and things

or **Introversion (I)**

Prefers to draw energy from the inner world of reflections, feelings and ideas

Sensing (S)

Prefers to focus on information gained from the five senses and on practical applications

or **Intuition (N)**

Prefers to focus on patterns, connections and possible meanings

Thinking (T)

Prefers to base decisions on logic and objective analysis of cause and effect

or **Feeling (F)**

Prefers to base decisions on a valuing process, considering what is important to people

Judging (J)

Likes a planned, organized approach to life, and prefers to have things decided

or **Perceiving (P)**

Likes a flexible, spontaneous approach and prefers to keep options open

Facing Changes

Key

SJ	SP	NT	NF
Sensing Judging	Sensing Perceiving	Intuition Thinking	Intuition Feeling

UNIT 13: BUSINESS LETTERS

Used to compliment your CV

Example 1

> 18 Sharp Street
> Warrington
> WA2 7EN
>
> Tel: 000000000
> Email
>
> 16 April 2013

Sue Young
HR Officer
Apple Mac
The Grange
Woolston
Cheshire
CH4 7DL

Dear Ms Young

Re: HR Manager Vacancy

With reference to the above advertisement in the Warrington Guardian, dated 16 April 2013, I have pleasure in submitting my CV for your attention.

I look forward to hearing from you with regards to an interview.

Yours sincerely

Karen Gould (Ms)

Enc: 1 *(this would be a copy of your CV)*

Informal Business Letter – Supporting Statement

18 Sharp Street
Warrington
Cheshire
WA2 7EN
Tel: 0000000000
Email

9 May 2013

Sue Smith
Director
Children's Trust
13 Oxford Street
Warrington
WA1 7EN

Dear Sue

Re: Fundraising Director

With reference to the above position and our conversation today, I have pleasure in enclosing my CV for your attention.

I have been working in the Public/Third Sector for 20 years within the Community and have worked at Management level in fundraising in the following areas:

- Donor – Gift and Corporate Fundraising – engaging local companies to donate gifts through setting-up of web and general Mail Shots – using databases;

also, contacting local and national entrepreneurs to contribute. This can be done through the National Lottery website.

- ESF, SRB, ERDF, LSC, JCP, Lottery, NRF etc. – I have been preparing bids for over 20 years and have had numerous successes and lately have managed to secure funding via ERDF, LSC, and ESF.

I work on a Fundraising Strategy based on the organisation's Business Plan reflecting 3-7 years and would act on Funding Alerts appropriate to the organisation.

I have secured many Lottery Bids and other funding through other organisations such as Lloyds TSB, Coalfields, NWDA, Tudor Trust, Esmee Foundation and so on.

This year I worked at Manchester Council as a Consultant in Commission/Project Management and supported advising the Third Sector in identifying additional funding streams.

I also use my organisational flair to organise Corporate Events and last year organised the 14-19 Diploma Agenda in Warrington for over 13,000 children and the year before coordinated the Homeless Charity Ball in Partnership with Warrington Wolves Rugby Club.

I am looking forward to taking our discussion further and displaying my suitability for the above post at an interview.

Yours sincerely

Karen Gould (Ms)
k.gould@hotmail.co.uk
(Mobile: 07906973032)

Enc: 1

The following are four different letters for four different types of approach:

In all cases, except for the chain letter, you should do your utmost to obtain the name, initials, title and mode of address (i.e. Mr, Mrs,Ms etc.) of the appropriate person to whom you will be writing.

- G Smith, HR Director. Dear Mr Smith is much more impressive than HR Director and Dear Sir – and in any case it could well be a Madam!

- Remember also that to go with the 'Reply to Advertisement' and probably the 'Targeted Speculative' letters you will need to 'tune' the standard CV that you are attaching in order to support your letter. This will usually involve modifying your personal profile, relisting your skills and achievements and altering the batting order of the bullet points concerning your last two jobs.

  In answer to a specific advertisement always read the details carefully, several times. Underline the skills and experience they are looking for. Then look to see if there are any other features which they do not mention but which might be applicable and where you have something to offer.

- Before responding, look up the company on the internet to see what useful information you can glean.

82 Chapel Lane
Warrington
Cheshire
CHE 3LX

Tel:01925
00000000
E mail:

8 September2013

M Smith
Director Human Resources
Blank Company Ltd
....
....

Dear Mr Smith

Vacancy for ....

I am responding to your advertisement in the
.... of ....

I enclose my CV from which you will notice that I match the specific criteria you are requiring, having the following relevant experience and skills............................. (keep this short –they can read the detail in the CV.)

May I also mention, since it would seem that your product has an international application, that I do speak fluent French, German and Spanish and have been resident in both France and Germany.

I look forward to meeting with you.

Yours sincerely

The So-Called Chain Letter

This is the type of letter you should write following a recommendation from a friend or colleague. ALWAYS do your utmost to leave the meeting with a name of someone else to whom you can write a similar letter.

As Above

Dear Mr Jones

I was talking recently to Charles Cornwall and he suggested that you would be someone who could be very helpful in giving me advice with respect to my future career direction.

I enclose my CV and really would be most grateful for a short amount of your time and for any advice and guidance you can give me.

I will ring you in a few days time to arrange a mutually convenient appointment.

Yours sincerely,

The Targeted Speculative Letter

This is for use where you have heard/read something about a company which leads you to believe that there might be an opening for someone with your skills.

As above

Name
Title
Address

Dear

I noticed from an article in yesterday's Daily Telegraph that your company has been successful in taking its products into the .... market and have recently taken on an additional....May I congratulate you on the results of your innovative approach.

Please find enclosed a copy of my CV because I believe that the skills and experience that I can offer may well be directly relevant to the further expansion of your business, specifically.... *(again keep this brief)*

I will ring you in a few days' time and would hope that we can arrange a short meeting to explore options.

Yours sincerely,

The Purely Speculative Letter

This is essentially 'flying a kite' to a company which, whilst not overtly advertising for staff at present, might be able to make use of your transferrable skills.

As above

Name
Title
Address

Dear ....

I am writing to you, enclosing my CV, in the hope that the skills and experience that I possess will be of use to your company.

In the light of my background, skills and achievements I feel that I could be of service in the role of, for example, ... but of course there may well be other relevant opportunities within your organisation.

I will ring you in a few days time to discuss what options might be available.

Yours sincerely

UNIT 14: E-MAIL ETIQUETTE RULES

Over the years I have unfortunately developed some bad email habits and it was only when at Manchester City Council, which has very strict rules on Email Etiquette, that I became aware of this. On several occasions my emails went into quarantine and I was once reprimanded! So, be aware.

I have been told on numerous occasions that one of my worst errors is using CAPITALS in the subject heading and too much in the content - thus SHOUTING!

One of the things I hate most is when people use 'War and Peace' dialogue to inform you of a simple piece of information.

WARNING

If you have a strange email address, eg: mickeymouse@hotmail.co.uk it will go into SPAM and thus sending your CV or any other piece of information re your Job Search is abortive before it starts.

For replies: always check your own SPAM box – just in case.

There are many etiquette guides and many different etiquette rules. Some rules will differ depending on whether you are a home or business user. Below we list what we consider are the most important email etiquette rules that apply to nearly all users:

Be concise and to the point

Do not make an email longer than it needs to be. Remember that reading an email is harder than reading printed communications and a long email can be very discouraging to read.

Use proper spelling, grammar and punctuation

This is not only important because improper spelling, grammar and punctuation give a bad impression, it is also important for conveying the message properly. Emails with no full stops or commas are difficult to read and can sometimes even change the meaning of the text. If your programme has a spell checking option, why not use it?

Answer swiftly

When people email a company, it is because they wish to receive a quick response. If they did not want a quick response they would send a letter or a fax. Therefore, each email should be replied to within at least 24 hours, and preferably within the same working day. If the email is complicated, just send an email back saying that you have received it and that you will get back to them. This will put the customer's mind at rest and usually customers will then be very patient.

Do not attach unnecessary files

By sending large attachments you can annoy people and even bring down their email system. Wherever possible try to compress attachments and only send attachments when they are productive. Moreover, you need to have a good virus scanner in place since people will not be very happy if you send them documents full of viruses.

Use proper structure and layout

Since reading from a screen is more difficult than reading from paper, the structure and layout is very important for email messages. Use short paragraphs and blank lines between each paragraph. When making points, number them or mark each point as separate to keep the overview.

Do not overuse the high priority option

We all know the story of the boy who cried wolf. If you overuse the high priority option, it will lose its function when you really need it. Moreover, even if mail has high priority, your message will come across as slightly aggressive if you flag it as 'high priority'.

Do not write in CAPITALS

IF YOU WRITE IN CAPITALS IT SEEMS AS IF YOU ARE SHOUTING. This can be highly annoying and might trigger an unwanted response in the form of a flame mail. Therefore, try not to send any email text in capitals.

Don't leave out the message thread

When you reply to an email, you must include the original mail in your reply, in other words click 'Reply', instead of 'New Mail'. Some people say that you must remove the previous message since this has already been sent and is therefore unnecessary. However, I could not agree less. If you receive many emails you obviously cannot remember each individual email. This means that a 'thread less email' will not provide enough information and you will have to spend a frustratingly long time to find out the context of the email in order to deal with it. Leaving the thread might take a fraction longer in download time, but it will save the recipient much more time and frustration in looking for the related emails in their inbox.

Add disclaimers to your emails

Business users should add disclaimers to internal and external mails, since this can help protect your company from liability. Consider the following scenario: an employee accidentally forwards a virus to a customer by email. The customer decides to sue your company for damages. If you add a disclaimer at the bottom of every external mail, saying that the recipient must check each email for viruses and that it cannot be held liable for any transmitted viruses, this will surely be of help to you in court. Another example: an employee sues the company for allowing a racist email to circulate the office. If your company has an email policy in place and adds an email disclaimer to every mail that states that employees are expressly required not to make defamatory statements, you have a good case of proving that the company did everything it could to prevent offensive emails.

Read the email before you send it

A lot of people don't bother to read an email before they send it out, as can be seen from the many spelling and grammatical mistakes contained in emails. Apart from this, reading your email through the eyes of the recipient will help you send a more effective message and avoid misunderstandings and inappropriate comments.

Do not overuse 'Reply to All'

Only use Reply to All if you really need your message to be seen by each person who received the original message.

Take care with abbreviations and emoticons

In business emails, try not to use abbreviations such as BTW (by the way) and LOL (laugh out loud). The recipient might not be aware of the meanings of the abbreviations and in business emails these are generally not appropriate. The same goes for emoticons, such as the smiley :-). If you are not sure whether your recipient knows what it means, it is better not to use it.

Be careful with formatting

Remember that when you use formatting in your emails, the sender might not be able to view formatting, or might see different fonts than you had intended. When using colours, use a colour that is easy to read on the background.

Take care with rich text and HTML messages

Be aware that when you send an email in rich text or HTML format, the sender might only be able to receive plain text emails. If this is the case, the recipient will receive your message as a .txt attachment. Most email clients however, including Microsoft Outlook, are able to receive HTML and rich text messages.

Do not request delivery and read receipts

This will almost always annoy your recipient before he or she has even read your message. Besides, it usually does not work anyway since the recipient could have blocked that function, or his/her software might not support it, so what is the use of using it? If you want to know whether an email was received it is better to ask the recipient to let you know if it was received.

Do not use email to discuss confidential information.

Sending an email is like sending a postcard. If you don't want your email to be displayed on a bulletin board, don't send it. Moreover, never make any libellous, sexist or racially discriminating comments in emails, even if they are meant to be a joke.

Use a meaningful subject

Try to use a subject that is meaningful to the recipient as well as yourself. For instance, when you send an email to a company requesting information about a product, it is better to mention the actual name of the product, e.g. 'Product A information' than to just say 'product information' or the company's name in the subject.

Avoid using URGENT and IMPORTANT

Even more so than the high-priority option, you must at all times try to avoid these types of words in an email or subject line. Only use this if it is a really, really urgent or important message.

Don't forward virus hoaxes and chain letters

If you receive an email message warning you of a new unstoppable virus that will immediately delete everything from your computer, this is most probably a hoax. By forwarding hoaxes you use valuable bandwidth and sometimes virus hoaxes contain viruses themselves, by attaching a so-called file that will stop the dangerous virus. The same applies to chain letters that promise incredible riches or ask your help for a charitable cause. Even if the content seems to be bona fide, the senders are usually not. Since it is impossible to find out whether a chain letter is real or not, the best place for it is the recycle bin.

NOTE:

Don't SHOUT in your email as though giving out instructions - I often do this though I do not mean to be rude but more to the point; sometimes my emails come across as being as though I am giving out orders. So, reading them beforehand is critical.

I personally, feel that emails are not an effective form of communication, which is why I always follow them up with a telephone call to arrange a meeting.

UNIT 15: PERSONAL PROFILES – A4/MINI

These are now in more use than ever and used in place of a CV. They are used normally for Professional/Executive Professionals. They come in two forms:

A4 – can be used in Social Media – LinkedIn; and Mini Profile, which are just a paragraph or two.

The A4 Profile with a Head Shot Photograph is your career history to date over the last 10 years featuring your significant achievements.

The Mini Profile just captures you – who you are – professional highlights to date.

PROFILE – Karen Melanie Gould – Accelerator High Growth Coach and Rockstar Mentor/ NW Business Angel – Author – Guest Speaker and Business Development Advisor and Professional/ Executive/Graduate Coach Careers. New for 2013: Government Mentoring Programme for Entrepreneurs – Funding/Workshops and Events for Rockstar Youth 2013 – Enterprise and Work Clubs NW – Franchise and E-learning development and a NEW for 2013-2014 - a very upmarket on-line Travel

Company for Professionals - a Community Platform 'GATEWAY' - E-Learning Social Enterprise based on Harvard Business on-line learning USA and as my role as an Investor have invested in a Comparison site and Hotel.

My main areas of expertise are:

Innovation – Business Development – Leadership & Management – Strategic Operations – Sales/ Marketing/PR – Travel Industry – IT/Cloud Platforms

During the 80s Karen worked in the Caribbean for the largest travel wholesaler in the world based in America as the Operations Director of the Caribbean until 1990, contracting with the largest hotel chains from Hilton to Sheraton etc., Ground Handling, Airport Operations, Events, Customer Service, FAMS, training of staff.

Prior to moving to Cheshire, Karen in the 90s had two businesses in the South East – a professional introduction company, Gold Introductions which was featured in many TV/radio/magazines and media productions and even starred in her own reality TV documentary on Channel 5, which went onto have a combined turnover of £3.4m together with a training and business development company – Advanced Training - securing contracts within the public sector and working in partnership with some of the top FTSE companies in the City re Training, Mentoring and Recruitment and having major contracts with Virgin and Saga etc.

In the early part of 2000, Karen worked in partnership with the Japanese Embassy supporting their top FTSE companies through training and recruitment re:graduates through her brokerage working with Panasonic andNumera Group etc.

INTERNATIONAL EXPERIENCE -

Since moving to the North West in 2002, Karen has recently expanded her international experience, contacts and processes in:

Malta – Regus/HSBC/Chamber of Commerce – Business Support Events/Guest Speaking

Italy – Overseas Business School – Sorrento/Milan – Business Student Exchange – Workshops – working with American and Russian Business Students

Sri Lanka – outsourcing staff for Cloud IT Companies and providing service support

Caribbean – outsourcing Customer Service Staff re: IT and Shell Graduate Scheme

South America/Spain – outsourcing IT Support Networks

Middle East - outsourcing IT Services re: staffing support, Customer Service, Sales/Marketing

Canada – Mentoring and Coaching Social Media Platforms

Brussels – Welfare to work – employability solutions

Spain – Travel and IT Industry.

ACHIEVEMENTS

2008 – UCLAN – Northern Lights Programme – Business Support – Outstanding Ofsted Report and UK Runner-Up SFEDI Award

2009 – Manchester City Council – UK Commissioning Award

2011 – Warrington Business Ventures, Business Woman for February

2011 – Runner-Up – Cheshire Woman of the Year

2011 – Nominate by Lord Wei – Big Society Award

2012 – UK Ambassador for Women in Enterprise

2012 – Rockstar Mentor for Business – have mentored in 2012 – 4 Millionaires

2012 – Business Angel NW

2013 – Business Mentor 18-30 Business Start Up – Rockstar Youth

2013 – Inspire4Women – Business Support for Women in Business - Santander

MOTIVATIONAL GUEST SPEAKER

Karen has been a Motivational Guest Speaker at various events, including theO2 Event in Liverpool

2010, Welfare to Work, 2012 Business NW Event, Manchester and Chester SME Event 2012 and Rockstar events. She has been invited to speak in USA, Brussels, Malta and Australia.

Karen Melonie Gould, ILM - Fellow/CMI/CIPD/MBA/BED
MINI PROFILE

MINI PROFILE– Karen Melonie Gould

In 2011 I delivered the BIS/JCP contracts for Professionals/Executives and for new businesses and also worked on various contracts from Bank of America to develop, sustain and grow existing businesses. Over the last four years on various projects I have supported over 150 businesses in the NW which have been supported by my Team of Mentors. I combined my Training/Mentoring with Guest Speaking which is supported by myself help books. *'Supporting Dreams'* was my practical guide to supporting a new business.

I am a UK Ambassador for Women's Enterprise and sit on the two Boards for Cheshire/Warrington for LEP re: Enterprise/BSU/Growth and Business Development.

I have launched for 2012 a WorkBiz Academy to reflect the demand for workshops by professionals and organisations to grow and develop with our support of Training and Mentoring.

Karen Melonie Gould

UNIT 16: APPLICATION FORMS

Most companies now prefer that you complete these online – so please do so as it could be a disadvantage for you if you don't. For example, if you are completing these for one Public Sector Council and then save it –for future reference for another application - you will only have to complete the Job Description / Specification section from fresh.

Hard Copies

These should be completed in **Black Fine Ink/Pen** and in **Block Capitals** where requested. It must be readable and legible so take your time and concentrate.

Have a hard copy of your CV to hand and on screen to cross check your dates etc.

Read the instructions through *carefully*, paying particular attention to the *job description* and *person specification* – check the latter against their checklist for essential points, so that you can complete all those tasks and provide evidence as an example. This will determine your suitability for the position by assessing your skills and qualifications. Please make these work related to be guaranteed an interview normally through a point system. This system is then carried over to the interview stage to score against a selection criteria as used in HR/Search & Selection/recruitment.

A presentation or a test could also be required to support this. PowerPoint is preferred now – so it is necessary to have these skills or develop your skills.

Psychometric testing could then be used too prior to interview selection or on the day of the interview (see Selby & Mills which is favoured by most public sector organisations and practise, practise, practise).

For each point assessed you can draw upon voluntary experience as an example- remember you are being assessed on your ability to do the job! Always give an example such as:

Good communication skills (rather than I have the ability to communicate – this is not sufficient)

As an experienced Trainer I have developed excellent communication skills through delivering training to diverse groups and from my presentations to corporate companies re donor fundraising; also, have conducted personal appraisals for internal staff.

Read through their advice on completing the form and use their checklist at the end to double check for enclosures before sending.

Example

Equal Opportunities Monitoring Form. Each company has clear policies on this and now **diversity** plays a big part– so please complete accurately and honestly.

Confidentiality/Discrimination Form. This is a workforce audit form and you must indicate any disabilities/medical conditions that could affect your work and to assist you at interview.

Ethnic Origin. Normally consistent with the ONS 2001 census.

Please make sure you put the job title and reference number on each form as sometimes they become separated from the main application form.

Personal Details

- Full name including any middle names, or names you have been known by in your professional life.

- Full postal address including your postal code.

- Contact details – include a land line and mobile number and a (professional) email address. Make sure they can contact you quickly to set up an interview.

You may have to provide your National Insurance number and date of birth – make sure these are correct. More recently there is a question relating to your residency and eligibility to work in this country and you may be asked to provide evidence at the interview stage. You may use a valid British Passport, your NI card or a Driving Licence but please check their requirements.

Education
Always in date order, most recent first and again you have your CV for this to copy from and check dates etc.

Training
Give relevant training details, most recent first. Use this to demonstrate your personal development and any professional bodies that you belong to.

Present Employer
If you are unemployed, put in voluntary work.

Make sure any salary, pay scale and dates are put in and when you can start – all indicate whether you are suitable for an interview.

Previous Work Experience
Date order with most recent first. Make sure it corresponds with your CV and explain any long gaps of 6 months or more.

Voluntary Work
Include any community work and working from home etc.

Criminal Background

Always give a Yes/No answer, never leave it blank and make sure you sign and date it. If you answer Yes, you need to check whether spent/unspent depending on the nature of the job. If in doubt, contact the HR/Line Manager of the Department to discuss in confidence.

Job Share

Indicate Yes/No – they sometimes have people listed who want job share.

Asylum and Immigration Act 1996

Do you have a work permit? Yes/No

Declaration

A signature is always required. Without signing and dating it – it is not valid.

NB: Most Application Forms are now requested online and details are captured and saved – for example with local councils, so read through carefully and ask someone to proofread it for you, especially the Job Description / Specification – have you nailed those **Essentials** as well as the **Desirables**? Evidence-based information should be taken from your last or most recent Job.

Business Letters to Support your Application Form

You will usually need a covering letter for your CV so we use a standard Business Informal letter style which is blocked and unpunctuated.

Again, use your spell check and ask someone to proofread it before you send it off.

In this exercise we aim to:

Eliminate those:

- spelling errors
- grammatical mistakes
- general untidiness.

Enhance your presentation:

- demonstrate attention to detail
- highlight those strengths
- showcase the pride you take in your work.

Do:

Make sure the letter supports the job description and highlight some of the words they have used within it and demonstrate your knowledge and experience of this in your letter.

Print off your letter, read it through several times or email it to a friend/mentor for suggestions.

This is your opportunity to say more in a supporting letter than is in your CV and demonstrate your IT and communication skills.

Don't:

Display any weaknesses – this states that you do not produce quality work or pay attention to detail.

Finally, it should be on one page and be to the point and factual.

The following pages contain a sample copy of a completed Application Form

Website: www.ljmu.ac.uk
Staff Application Form

This form is available in alternative formats e.g. Braille, large print, disc and on-line

To enable us to process your application, this form and the Equal Opportunity form must be completed and returned by the closing date to Personnel, Liverpool John Moores University, Rodney House, 70 Mount Pleasant, Liverpool L3 5UX. (Email: - jobs@ ljmu.ac.uk). Can you please?

- Complete the form legibly using black ink, biro or typeset

- Write the vacancy reference number and candidate number on all pages as the front sheet may be detached from the form. Please ensure any supporting documents are on A4 sheets and securely attached to this form.

Please note the University requires a completed application form.

Post Applied For	HEAD OF EMPLOYABILITY & UNDERGRADUATE BUSINESS AND MANAGEMENT PROGRAMMES				
Vacancy Ref	IRC172	Candidate No (if known)			

Section 1   Personal Details

Title (Mr, Mrs, Ms Dr etc)	MS	Surname/ Family Name	GOULD	
First Name(s)	KAREN MELONIE			
Address for correspondence	0 ANY STREET WARRINGTON CHESHIRE			
Postcode	WA2 7EN	Email Address		k.gould@hotmail.co.uk

We may need to contact you by phone. If this is acceptable please give the phone numbers where you can be reached or where messages can be left.

Daytime Contact no	079391 64110	Evening Contact no	

Are you aged 65 or over or does your 65th birthday fall within 6 months of the date of your application? Yes No

Work Permit	
Do you need a work permit to work in the UK?	Yes ☐ No ☒

(UK and EU/EEA citizens do not require work permits) Original documents will be required in the event of an employment offer being made.

Disability

Applications are welcome from disabled people. Do you have a disability that you wish the panel to take into consideration? Where candidates meet the essential criteria appropriate arrangements can be made for an interview. Please give details of any particular requirements

N/A

Application Form for Staff Appointment

Vacancy Reference		Candidate Number	

<u>Section 2</u>   <u>References</u>

All offers of employment are subject to satisfactory references and medical clearance. Please give details of 2 people to whom references may be made, one of who should be your current or most recent employer. Please tell us clearly whether or not we may contact your referees.

	Referee 1	Referee 2
Name	JULIA STICKLEY	DAVID MOWAT
Designation	NORTHERN LIGHTS PROGRAMME MANAGER	CONSERVATIVE PARTY MP - WARRINGTON SOUTH
Address (including postcode)	UCLAN MEDIA FACTORY PRESTON PR1 6ED	CONSERVATIVE ASSOCIATION STRETTON STREET WARRINGTON AW4 1EN
Tel No	00 000 0000	00 000 0000
Fax No		
Email	Jstickley@anynetwork	dmowat@anynetwork
May not be contacted before Interview (please tick)	☐	☐

Checklist

Please ensure that you have either entered/ completed:

1	Vacancy Number on all pages of the application form	☒
2	Candidate Number (if known) on all pages of the application form	☒
3	Relevant sections of the application form with signature and date	☒
4	Equal Opportunity Monitoring Form	☒
5	Clearly indicated whether we contact referees	☒

6	Attached supporting documents (excluding CV) Please specify:	☒

NB Please note the University requires a completed application form.

Official Use	References Sought	
	Disability Needs	

Comments: please use box below to give us comments on how this form can be improved

Application Form for Staff Appointment

Vacancy Reference		Candidate Number	

Section 3   Education and Training

	Dates	Title/Subject/Grade/Class of Degree Qualification Reg No (e.g. Teaching, Nursing)
GCSE, A' level or equivalent School/College attended: -BENNETT MEMORIAL DIOCESAN SCHOOL FOR GIRLS WEST KENT COLLEGE	1977-79	GCSE's **ENGLISH LANGUAGE/ LITERATURE ARITHIMATIC, BUSINESS STUDIES, COMMERCE CHRISTIAN FAITH**
HNC/D/Foundation/First Degree Awarding Institution: REDHILL HIGHER EDUCATION COLLEGE	1985	**FURTHER EDUCATION TEACHERS CERTIFICATE COURSE - CREDIT**
Higher Degree(s) Awarding Institution: BRIGHTON UNIVESITY	2000	**CIPD LEVEL**
CHESTER UNIVERSITY	2008/09	**MA BUSINESS MANAGEMENT TO COMPLETE**
Professional Qualifications (if any) Awarding Body: ILM	2009	**TUTOR/MEMBER/ TRAINER - DIPLOMA LEVEL 5 - LEADERSHIP - MANAGEMENT - MENTORING -COACHING**

Other training	2008-09	LEVEL 3 TRAINERS CERTIFICATE - SAMVOLUNTEER MANAGEMENT DIPLOMA - COACHING PERSONAL/ BUSINESSD
Leading to qualifications CITY & GUILDS - TRAINING CERFICATES		
Membership	2009	
Details of other training or memberships of professional bodies relevant to your application ILM		

Research Publications

Where appropriate please attach a separate list of your publications and/or research interests with this form. Please clearly indicate the Vacancy Reference and Candidate Number (if known)

Application Form for Staff Appointment

Vacancy Reference	IRC172	Candidate Number	

Section 4   Employment Details

Current or Most Recent Employment			
Employer Name & Address	**Position and Duties**	**Employment Details**	
CONSERVATIVE ASSOCIATION PARTY WARRINGTON	BUSINESS/JOB SEARCH CONSULTANT - WROTE AND DELIVERED JOB SDEARCH AND BUSINESS PROGRAMME - ACHIEVED 10/13 INTO EMPLOYMENT	From	JAN 09 - PRESENT
		To	PRESENT
		Current/Last Salary	£00 per hour
		Leaving Reason	CAREER ADVANCEMENT
		Notice Period	N/A

....

Past Employment			
Employer Name & Address	**Position and Duties**	**Employment Details**	
MANCHESTER CITY COUNCIL	COMMISSIONING/ PROJECT MANAGER - MANAGED 20 ORGANISATIONS - BUDGETS OF OVER £4M -BUDGETS - REPORTS AND SET UP COMMISSIONING MODEL FOR MCC	From	NOV 08
		To	APR 09
		Leaving Reason	TEMP POSITON

Past Employment			
Employer Name & Address	**Position and Duties**	**Employment Details**	
UCLAN MEDIA FACTORY PRESTON	**BUSINESS CONSULTANT - SUPPORTED 5/6 BUSINESSNES IN 08 INTO SME AND DEVELOPMENT THROUGH MENTORING AND TRAINING AND WRITING BIDS**	From	**JAN 07**
		To	**PRESENT**
		Leaving Reason	**CAREER DEVELOPMENT**

Employer Name & Address	**Position and Duties**	**Employment Details**	
YMCA WARRINGTON	**FUNDRAISING/BUSINESS DEVELOPMENT MANAGER - CREATED SUBSTAINABILITY THROUGH BUSINESS DEVELOPMENT AND FUNDING FOR 3YEARS**	From	**MAR 07**
		To	**APR 08**
		Leaving Reason	**CAREER DEVELOPMENT**

Employer Name & Address	**Position and Duties**	**Employment Details**	
MANCHESTER CITY COUNCIL MANCHESTER	**EDUCATION SENIOR COMMUNICATIONS OFFICER - LIASING WITH ALL EDUCATIONAL ESTABLISHMENTS RE CUSTOMER SERVICE**	From	**APR 07**
		To	**MAR 08**
		Leaving Reason	**TEMP POSITION**

Application Form for Staff Appointment

Vacancy Reference	IRC172	Candidate Number	

Section 5   Further Information

Further Information

Please use this section to provide evidence of how you meet the person specification and job description criteria. The person specification details the experience, knowledge and abilities, which are necessary to carry out the job.

I have true entrepreneurai blood in my veins, coming from a family history of having their own successful businesses. Indeed these skills and this experience has enabled me to have had 3 companies - a TRAINING & DEVELOPMENT COMPANY - A SOCIAL NETWORKING COMPANY and a Consultancy in SME Business Development and Mentoring. So, I intend to adopt an approach which demonstrates innovation which has created growth for myself and whilst at UCLAN as a Business Mentor created business development for 5/6 of my origianl start-ups.

I can demonstrate a credible change management skill, which is hands on and being that I am a good strategist - work to various methods of strategy from Business Plans - Marketing Plans to having an every day ACTION PLAN - incorporating STAFF DEVELOPMENT through Training and regular communications - whether it is weekly team meetings - email or team building excercises from WORK SHOPS etc.

I set myself goals and set my team-orientated goals and indivudal goals through Appraisals and working to a BUSINESS PLAN/STRATEGY plan ahead and incorporate an element or risk or a continency plan within the BUSINESS PLAN to engage and comfort any problems before they happen - this allows you then to Plan through Budgets. Whilst at MCC - I was responsible for the budgets of 21 projects - £4M and used SAP re Budgets which has 'flag ups' and DASHBOARD to monitor progress and outcomes - these type of tools enable you to plan ahead and keep within budgets.

I have extensive networking contacts, as I personally attend rather a lot of events and meetings in Liverpool - Chester - Manchester - Preston and the North West in general. I attend BUSINESS NETWORK EVENTS - SOCIAL ENTERPRISE EVENTS - E-MARKETING EVENTS - DWP EVENTS and so on - so I have created for myself a database/portoflio of contacts from Educational to Business Links.

I am highly motivated and inspire and motivate others, that is one of the reasons I am able to deliver high outcomes. I have storng leadership skills which I use to influence and persuade to win and secure contracts and form partnerships and new stalkholders. Indeed, whilst working at Liverpool Vision -through events - I have maintained those contacts which I have found supportive over the last few years.

i am a very creative person having created many TRAINING PROGRAMMES from more recently creating a HIGHER EXECUTIVE/ GRADUATE TRAINING PROGRAMME in Warrington - achieved 10/13 into employment and this programme will now be dilvered within Warrington for the next year. Also, your WOW Programme showed a interest in this and I have been in contact with the team there.

I solve problems by facing them before they happen and always have contingency plans to overcome any milstones or barriers. Indeed, whilst deliverying the Job Programme - for the next year which will be more gratuate orientated - some of the units have been modified to reflect this - ie - more - e-marketing and soft skills to be added and developed.

I have outstanding interpersonal skills and this will be evident at an interview, but is imperative when working as part of a team as I did at MCC - in a team 20 -where we supported each other.

I have worked in and around employment for the last 20 years and from this experence have a good understanding on how to improve employability. So, on this last course - I introduced a 3 prong attach - BUSINESS MENTORING - PERSONAL EFFECTIVENESS and enabling to coach along and support those unemployed.

Having been recently working at UCLAN with my own HUB - I understand how to work in a modern student centre and the approach required to improve their employablity from increasing awareness of e-marketing - soft skills and recording interactive tasks for students to learn from - it is all about user lead learning which motivates them and puts the responsibility on them to support their own development.

I have a FETC - CREDIT - CIPD - exam not taken due to illness - ILM APPROVED TUTOR/TRAINER - various training - coaching - mentoring and management certificates and have been accepted to complete my MA BUSINESS ADMINSTRATION at Chester 09 - was accepted last year - but course was cancelled due to numbers. I have also shown an interest in your BA RISK MANAGEMENT COURSE at LJMU as a continegency plan.

I believe strongly that my experience - skills and expertise could take this role to another level and I am looking forward to be contacted for an interview.

PLEASE NOTE: I AM ON HOLIDAY 3/17 August 09.

PLEASE CONTINUE ON A SEPARATE SHEET IF NECESSARY, clearly stating Vacancy Reference and Candidate Number (if known)

Application Form for Staff Appointment

Vacancy Reference		Candidate Number	

Section 6   Further Information

Criminal Convictions

Certain posts are exempt from the rehabilitation of Offenders Act 1974. Applicants for such posts are required to declare all criminal convictions, spent or unspent. This includes any posts where the post holder is likely to have access to children, sick or disabled people (e.g. any posts based on hospital premises) and posts where there is the potential for fraud (e.g. chartered or certified accountants). **This list is not, however, exhaustive and for posts, which fall under the exemption, this will be indicated in the further particulars for the post.** Applicants for such posts must complete the following information.

Have you any criminal convictions (unspent or pending) Yes ☐   No ☒

If yes, please give brief details:

Note: the successful applicant for any post exempt from the Rehabilitation of Offenders Act 1974 will be required to give consent for the University to check with the Criminal Records Bureau for the existence and content of any criminal record. Information received from the police will be kept in strict confidence and will be destroyed once the University is satisfied in this regard.

Relationship (if any) with any member of the University staff or Governor	

Canvassing or failure to disclose a relationship to a Governor or employee of LJMU will disqualify your application. Please declare any such relationship.

Please state where you saw the advertisement	

Section 7   Declaration

I confirm that all the information provided, including supplements is correct and understand that any false statement could result in an offer of employment being withdrawn or in termination of employment.

(If sending this form electronically pleases type your name in the signature box below to indicate you have read and agree with this declaration.)

Signature   **KAREN GOULD**   Date   22 July 09

Data protection Act 1998: Some of the data which is given on this form will be entered onto a computer database for the purpose of recruitment administration and equal opportunity monitoring. All application forms except for the appointed candidate will be shredded after 6 months in compliance with University policy.

Please note that all appointments are subject to receipt of satisfactory references and medical clearance and/or risk assessment. Some posts may be subject to a police check.

For Official Use Only

Please ask candidate to provide telephone number where they may be contacted following the interview.

Name of Candidate   Tel No.:
Name   0700 000000 or please email
                                       response

UNIT 17: THE HIDDEN JOB MARKET

Based on Chris Cardell's Sunday Times and BBC appearances on entrepreneurial success, this marketing strategy aims to increase your business success from 50% to 250%.

Top Ten Tips

1. Stop wasting time – do not rely on advertisements; there is the **Hidden Job Market** to follow up.

2. Be strong and persuasive in your:
    - CV
    - Letters
    - Personal statement
    - Interview technique
    - Confirmation/Contract.

3. Build trust, be likeable, add interest.

4. Direct response. Richard Branson states that **you** represent yourself, **you** are your own brand; look at your business cards, letterheads, email accounts etc. - they should be professional and have a signature at the end for communications. Use the telephone for

introducing yourself – this is me and this is what I do!

5. Use internet markets such as Google. This is the biggest breakthrough in the last century - it allows you to reach out to people and to research them.

Register your CV with CV sites, eg.Monster and Total Jobs etc.; recruitment agencies such as Morgan Hunt and Reed Professionals; social networking sites such as Face book, Twitter, LinkedIn and even the national press have their own email alerts, such as Telegraph Jobs.

6. Have a traceable, factual, work history and references. Deliver and reassure based on trust and honesty.

7. What's in it for me? Is that being selfish? We think the whole world revolves around us. Think of the quality of the service you give, the benefits to the company – Learn their needs and understand their history.

8. Have a strategy – be organised, have a work plan.

9. Follow up. Don't give up - and try again and again. If they have shown an interest, then every month follow this up. 60% of people move on and this creates more vacancies.

10. Don't sell yourself cheap! Only 20% of employers make decisions based on price.

Marketing in today's job market: WHAT WE DO NOW

- Job adverts in newspapers/journals
- Job sites/vacancies on weekly sites – local councils etc.
- Job alerts – join alerts from agencies and business links
- Agencies – specialist agencies
- Word of mouth – friends and family
- Job fairs
- Networking events
- Tenders/bids
- Auctions.

Hidden job market: WHAT YOU WILL DO NOW

- Keeping contacts in your industry – follow up with a coffee;
- Canvass companies that demonstrate growth – new contracts – profits – success stories in local press and in the Media;
- Attend functions/events – Network Events;

- Email/telephone people/organisations in your industry that have recently been in the national/local press to compliment them and ask for advice;

- Word of mouth: let people know, via a monthly email, that you are available and let them recommend you!

- **LinkedIn.com** -This is the way forward; ask your friends and colleagues to join the above and then join the Groups Section of your industry.

I have it on the highest authority that due to the ever-increasing costs of advertisements and the % fee for recruitment agencies, employers use a **search engine** or engage someone in HR or even hire agencies that specialise using LinkedIn to find the suitable candidate and save the employer the time, resources and expense and they do look at potential applicants with a recommendation.

The answer here lies in Social Media. Since using LinkedIn four years ago I have elevated my employment opportunities by 70%.

UNIT 18: SOCIAL MEDIA-INTRODUCTION

Third Marketing have pulled together the following glossary of Social Media terms. Whether you are a social media guru or you haven't got the slightest idea what a 'tweet' is, we hope that you find this compilation useful.

Alerts - Alerts can be set up for various terms or phrases to notify an individual whenever those terms appear on the internet in newly published content. Alerts are usually sent to an individual via email.

Blog - Blogs are websites hosting content that is self-published, typically by the owner of the site (blogger). Blogs keep a record of all content updates which are posted to the site in reverse chronological order (thus the original term, web-logs). Visitors can view the updates on the site or on an aggregator, via RSS feeds.

Bookmarking - Bookmarking means to save a website address for future reference. This can be done individually on an internet browser. An address can also be bookmarked through a social bookmarking site, such as del.icio.us. Social bookmarking allows visitors to comment on and rate the content that is stored there. Other social bookmarking sites include Digg, Stumble Upon and Mixx.

Del.icio.us - Del.icio.us is a popular social bookmarking site which allows members to share, store and organise their favourite online content.

Digg - Digg is a popular social bookmarking and crowd sourcing site.

Facebook.com - Face book is a popular social networking site which is free access. Face book was initially limited to students with a college email domain but has since expanded to be available to anyone 13 years of age or older.

Flickr - Flickr is a media hosting network where users can upload and share image files.

Forums - Forums are areas on a website which are dedicated to facilitating conversation through comments and message boards.

Friends - Friends, or connections, are individuals who agree to link to one another's profile on a social networking site, such as Face book or MySpace.

Groups - Groups are micro-communities within a social networking site for individuals who share a particular interest.

Guru.com - Guru is a freelance marketplace. It allows companies to find freelance workers for commissioned work.

Hash tag # - Hash tags are placed in front of words to tag or categorise a post. Hash tags are used on Twitter to group tweets and more easily follow discussion topics.

LinkedIn.com - LinkedIn is a social networking site. Much like Face book, LinkedIn allows members to connect with other users on the network, although LinkedIn is geared more **toward professional connections.**

Meetup.com - Meetup.com is an online social networking portal that facilitates offline group meetings in various localities around the world. Meetup allows members to find and join groups unified by a common interest, such as politics, books, games, movies, health, pets, careers or hobbies. Users enter their city and the topic they want to meet about, and the website helps them arrange a place and time to meet. Topic listings are also available for users who only enter a location.

Micro-blog - A micro-blog is a social media utility where users can share small status updates and information. Micro-blogs combine aspects of blogs (personalised web posting) and aspects of social networking sites (making and tracking connections, or 'friends').

Mixx - Mixx is a user-driven social media website that serves to help users submit or find content by peers based on interest and location.

MySpace - MySpace is a social networking community. MySpace allows more freedom for users to personalise their profiles than other social networking sites, such as Face book, which are more structured.

Peer-to-peer - Peer-to-peer refers to any type of interaction between two or more people within a specific social network. Often the term is associated with file sharing.

Podcast - A podcast is audio or video content which can be downloaded and listened to or viewed offline. Podcasts are often created to provide copies of radio or television programming, as well as to accompany internet press releases.

Profile - A profile is a personal page within a social network created by a user. The profile provides information about the user and often links to the profiles of the user's friends.

Registration - Registration refers to the process of signing up to participate in an online social media network or community.

RSS - RSS stands for Really Simple Syndication (or Rich Site Summary). RSS feeds allow users to subscribe to content updates on their favourite blogs and websites.

Slideshare.net - SlideShare is the world's largest community for sharing presentations. Individuals and organisations upload presentations to share their ideas, connect with others, and generate leads for their businesses. Anyone can find presentations on topics that interest them. They can tag, download, or embed presentations into their own blogs and websites.

Social Media - Social media refers to all online tools that are available for users to generate content and communicate through the internet. This includes blogs, social networks, file hosting sites and bookmarking sites.

Social Network - A social network is a site or community on the internet where members can interact with one another and share content.

StumpleUpon - StumbleUpon is an internet community that allows its users to discover and rate web pages, photos and videos.

Subscribing - Subscribing is the process of adding an RSS feed to an aggregator.

Tags - Tags are a list of keywords which are attached to bookmarked content, a blog post or a media file. The tags are used to help categorize the content.

Tweet - A tweet refers to an entry made on the micro-blogging site, Twitter. Tweets can be status updates, informative or even include links and can be up to 140 characters long.

Twitter.com - Twitter is a micro-blogging platform which allows users to create profiles and follow other users as friends, much like a social networking site.

VisualCV.com - Visual CV is a free multimedia online CV site that allows you to add images, charts, references, awards and much more.

Finding a Job through Social Media

Everyone knows that job candidates are flooding the market right now. There are jobs out there, but standing out in a sea of experienced, qualified applicants can be difficult, but not impossible. Social media offers a plethora of opportunities for marketers to reach consumers and businesses, but it also offers job candidates a direct line of communication to corporations and hiring managers. Here are some tips for would-be new hires - both to standing out in the crowd and to finding the job opportunities leveraging social media:

1. **Clean Up Your Online Image.** First and foremost, make sure that your online image is Google-ready. Most hiring managers will Google a job candidate at some point in the hiring process - sometimes before an interview. Google yourself and find out what happens. Is your LinkedIn profile up to date? Has your personal blog been dormant for months? Do photos from a night of over indulging in Cancun come up in search

results? Take a good inventory of how you appear online and prepare the groundwork. Make sure that content that a potential employer can access is appropriate. Use privacy settings whenever possible. Untag yourself in photos if you can't remove them from the public eye. Ask people to recommend you on sites that allow reviews such as LinkedIn and Guru.com. Create new 'favorable' content to hit the top of the search results (see next tip).

2. **Make Yourself 'Findable'.** If you don't have an online presence, you need one. Social media is a great way to quickly create an online reputation for yourself and build up your resume and profile. Most of the tools are free. Create a LinkedIn profile, a Face book page, join Twitter and any relevant professional networks or communities in your field. Even adding your name to a directory or commenting on a high profile blog can create new content for a prospective employer to find when searching for information on you. You can create a YouTube video of yourself (but make sure it's industry/job appropriate) or a full website resume.

3. **Be an Expert.** In addition to looking for job opportunities, you should be looking

for opportunities to put your skills into action. Consider starting a blog, or at least a guest blog, to highlight your field of knowledge. Create an online portfolio of your work with a Flickr account. If you are a marketer, answer questions on LinkedIn pertaining to marketing (this also puts your name and business smarts in front of all of your connections).Participate in message boards and forums that are frequented by prospective employers and be a helpful presence - answer questions, post articles, start discussions, etc. Focus your 'tweets' on Twitter to build a following in your field. Share your ideas, best practices, relevant articles and other information that 'prove' you are in the know and have up to date skills to share. Post PowerPoint presentations on SlideShare to show off your handiwork.

4. **Join the Group.** Groups on LinkedIn, Face book and other platforms offer more opportunities to connect with potential employers and colleagues. When you join a group on LinkedIn, you are often able to message members directly. This can be a direct line of communication to a hiring manager or executive at the firm of your desire. When appropriate, you can also post a message to the entire group to help in your job search. In addition to groups,

a single connection may be your gateway to the right job opportunity. Leverage individual connections to facilitate introductions to hiring managers.

5. **Actively Listen.** Don't just rely on the traditional job boards to find your next position. Set up RSS feeds and Google Alerts to notify you when new jobs have been posted in your field. Check out non-traditional job boards. For example, LinkedIn also has job boards inside group settings where only group members can post job opportunities. If you 'fan' a company on Face book, you might be the first to find out about job openings. Seek out and follow recruiters (professional recruiters and internal hiring managers) on Twitter. Many often post job opportunities on Twitter first before sending out mass communications to their network. In addition, responding via Twitter may separate you from the 'death by inbox' syndrome that plunges many resumes into the email abyss.

6. **Turn Online Connections Into Offline Connections.** Social media offers us opportunities to expand our Dunbar Number (theoretical number of sustainable social relationships that one person can maintain) from 150 to

hundreds of thousands. However, when it comes to getting a job, candidates are usually only hired after they've met the hiring manager in person. And, influencers still tend to recommend candidates that they know and have met directly. So, take your online relationships offline. Participate in networking events, organize a MeetUp, take a connection out to lunch and ask for informational interviews to get some face-time with potential employers.

UNIT 19: LINKED IN

The recent LinkedIn profile updates may seem subtle at first glance, but to stay current on this professional social networking site, there are some things you should know and do.

First, be prepared to get a professional head shot, given that your smiling face is much more prominent as a result of the updated look that LinkedIn has fully rolled out.

Wayne Breitbarth, LinkedIn consultant and author of <u>The Power Formula for LinkedIn Success</u>, reminds us that this isn't Face book–LinkedIn is all about professionalism and credibility. It's important to stay current on your profile and give your contacts what they are looking for.

Breitbarth stepped in to help with that task by providing this review of the LinkedIn profile changes and simple tips to help you stand out. Breitbarth's pointers might take only minutes to execute but will deliver a powerful impression. Here's how:

1. **Put more emphasis on your profile photo.** LinkedIn is putting the focus on your face with a larger profile image.

This means you had better have a photo, and it had better be good, now more than ever. Stick with a simple head shot, dressed as you would when meeting a client. People want to do business with people they like, and your photo is the first impression; make it professional and likeable!

2. **Take advantage of what's no longer featured.** Gone are the number of recommendations and the full synopsis of your work and educational experience. And your websites are no longer prominently displayed on your profile page. This means that LinkedIn users need to take greater advantage of the other profile features to make this information more visible.

3. **Work on your headline–it's more important than ever!** Because the amount of information in your top box has been reduced, the remaining information is more important than ever, including your headline. The 120-character headline is one of the best spots on your profile to explain your brand. You'll want to include your most important keywords as well. Your current job title will be shown in the top box only if you have just one. However, if you have multiple current jobs, only the company names will be displayed,

not your titles. In this case, consider the keywords by which you want to be found. If the job title is relevant, include it in the headline.

4. **Also note: The summary section is much more prominent.** Because of the reduced size of the top box, your summary is now above the fold; thus more important, especially the first few sentences. Those sentences had better pack a punch relating to your current business objectives and your credibility.

5. **Treat 'contact information' like a business card.** This information used to be in various spots on the old version of your profile page. Now it is summarised nicely in the top box and opens after a person clicks the Contact Info tab right next to the picture of the index card. Be sure to include all the ways you feel comfortable with people contacting you. Available options are websites, Twitter, email, phone, IM, and your address.

6. **Consider that website addresses are harder to find.** The websites included on your profile (you can list up to three) were previously quite prominent, but now they are a bit hidden in the Contact Info section. Thus, you may want to mention your website(s) in your summary and in the description(s) of

your job experience. This will not be a clickable link, but at least a person can find it without having to open the Contact Info tab.

So, smile for the camera, update your new profile page, and leverage your LinkedIn experience and relationships to build your business.

Joining groups of like-minded people can also expand your LinkedIn network. If you would like to join with other small and medium sized business owners, Business Matters has a dedicated LinkedIn group.

LinkedIn Tips

- Use the free version to start
- Try to have a 100% profile
- Grow a valuable network, don't be a Lion - someone that does not share - Ask for recommendations
- Search companies you would like to work for, who works for them, what groups are they in
- Join and contribute to groups
- Use the Job Search section
- Ask contacts for a heads-up on jobs they know about
- Get your skills and experience endorsed.

UNIT 20: HOW TO FIND A JOB ON TWITTER

Tough economic times call for innovative approaches and with the unemployment rate on the rise, how do you find career opportunities fast? One great option is Twitter. Twitter is evolving as another resource, in addition to traditional methods, for both job searching and recruiting. Why not follow the steps below:-

1. **Make your Twitter presence 'employer-friendly'**

    - Put your job pitch in your Twitter bio (which is 160 characters)

    - Use a professional looking avatar

    - Tweet about your job search.

2. **Utilize your Twitter background**. There is a great deal of space you can use to promote yourself. Don't know how to create a professional-looking Twitter background? Use the free template to design your own.

3. **Include a link to an online CV** or resume in your bio. Use a tool like Visual CV.

4. **Establish yourself as an expert** in your field on Twitter. It's important to note that you should **not** misrepresent yourself. If you're not a medical doctor, don't play one on Twitter. As those on Twitter become interested in your content, when employers are looking at you, you'll have more than just your resume to back up your knowledge and experience.

How do you get to know the right people? It's not always about who you're looking for; some people on Twitter are actually looking for YOU. There are many job recruiters who use Twitter to look for potential candidates. Before contacting a recruiter via Twitter, check out:

- Their bio
- Follower/Following ratio (Have they been around a while? Do they follow people back?)
- Click the link to their website
- Ask others in your network whether or not the recruiter is a credible source.

Job Search Tools and Resources

A reactive job search on Twitter probably isn't the best way to find a job. There are many new Twitter tools and applications to assist with a proactive job search.

@Microjobs - Started by well-known PR professional, Brian Solis, @Microjobs was developed to bring together job seekers and recruiters through tweets. Recruiters begin their tweets with @Microjobs, and then submit. The @Microjobs account automatically tweets out requests to its growing network of job seekers.

TweetMyJobs - Another tool born out of Twitter for job seekers and recruiters. Follow the hashtag#Tweetmyjobs and visit the website. This is a very simple (and free) tool for job seekers. You can subscribe to desired job channels and even have new openings automatically sent to your mobile phone. Even better -you can specify which cities you want notifications from.

Job search accounts

There is a variety of Twitter accounts dedicated to providing job listings by field, company, region, and more. Here are just a few to get you started:

- @thirdsectorjobs – Jobs in the Voluntary Sector

- @sciencejobs_UK – Jobs within the Sciences

- @twitjobs – range of sectors advertising a multitude of roles

- @JobMote_Ruby – recruitment agency based in Manchester
- @Warringtonjobs – Jobs within the Warrington Area
- @jobworld – recruitment agency operating throughout the UK.

To find additional Twitter job resources, use the Twitter search function and type in keywords such as 'job openings', 'looking for a job', or 'healthcare career'. Your next job could be just a tweet away. *Source:Mashable*

Twitter Tips

- Have separate personal and professional accounts, good bio and photo;
- Follow people, companies and institutions relevant to your career choice;
- Use 'who to follow' for list of people and companies being followed by those you are following;
- Use # search for threads such as #jobs #hiring #recruiting;
- Sign up to Tweetmyjobs.com;
- Don't spam.

UNIT 21: FACEBOOK

Using Face book in your Job Search

Social Media is a hot commodity in every industry; more and more companies are using social media in order to boost their brand.

Personally, I do not like Face book and only use it once a week to post an advert for an event of mine or to update on a significant achievement in my professional life from the last week.

Socialising via Face book can be quite dangerous and I find that people who you once dated in your teens under the influence of alcohol seem to find you and claim their long lost love for you.

I am aware though, that most companies have a Face book page and do recruit through this and always track what their employees have been up to. So, be aware NOT TO post pictures of yourself falling out of a club whilst on holiday or say something detrimental about your employers.

Employers who have used this form of social media have been known to use Face book to find an excuse to get rid of you, particularly if on a probation for 6 months.

It is thought to be the most used form of social media for 18-30 year olds and while working on the www.rockstaryouth.co.ukEntrepreneur Programme in 2013 this is the one that most of our referrals came from - so for marketing for this age group it is ideal.

Many are also using it when looking to hire new employees.

Face book now has over 500 million users, with over 250 million logging on every day. With Face book as the most visited site on the web it is not hard to see how useful it can be in your job search.

Friends and Networks

The simplest way of finding a job on Face book is asking: ask your friends, family and networks if they know of any available positions. This way they know that you are looking and can keep an eye out for you. It can be daunting or embarrassing for some people to ask for a job but sometimes it boils down to 'if you don't ask, you don't get'.

Pages

Face book pages are growing daily with companies looking to reach out to their customers. Actively 'Like' and follow companies that you would be willing to work for. You will find that they will announce if they have any vacancies. Again, there's no harm in asking if they have any available positions. There are some job and location specific Face book pages which will give you a greater chance of finding a job in your area of expertise and your local area.

Marketplace

Marketplace has a dedicated job section with over 100,000 jobs being advertised. This is a great place to find jobs in your local area or all over the country and do so in a more personal manner. Most recruiters will use their personal Face book accounts to post jobs; as a result if you reply to the post they will be able to see your public profile. Which leads us on to...

Privacy Settings

Face book has been taking privacy a lot more seriously recently, and this is a sign that you should be too. With reports of staff being fired because of a simple Face book update occurring almost daily, it's crucial that you lockdown your profile from prying eyes.

Here are a few simple rules:

- **Choose a suitable profile picture** – Yes, you can show yourself having fun, but don't choose something that crosses the line.

- **Ensure only friends** can view your wall, status updates and pictures – it's the easiest way to ensure information gets out only to the people you want to see it.

- **Groups** – This is a great way to group certain people, whether it's work, family or friends. Creating groups allows you to send messages to just one particular group.

During these tough economical times job seekers must use every tool available to them to stand out from the crowd. Hopefully this article has given you some ideas on how to utilise everything Face book has to offer.

Face book Tips

- Leverage your friends
- Research and interact with companies
- Search using terms like 'Recruiting' and 'Recruitment'
- Face book Marketplace
- Face book link searches e.g. Adzuna. co.uk

Don't forget to 'Like' our Facebook page **to stay up to date with our latest news and views** www. workbizacademy.co.uk.

UNIT 22: BLOGGING FOR JOB SEARCH

If you're considering entering the world of guest blogging, here are a few tips I have learned that might be helpful to you:

- **Play by the rules.** Many blogs have established guidelines that they require their guest bloggers to follow. Reading, understanding, and following these rules is essential to guest blogging. It's like when visiting someone else's home, you must follow the rules of their house (even if they are different from your own) in order to be asked back again. The same idea applies in the blogging world.

- **Be prepared for edits**. As a writer, I'm sure you are very protective of your work and when others try and change it, it can feel like a personal attack. If a blog wants to edit your piece, don't take it personally. Sometimes another pair of eyes catches something you might have missed and they end up making your work better! If edits are made, read through them with an open mind and if something was changed that you don't approve of, approach the blog with an even temper and ask to discuss the changes.

- **Don't assume anything.** If you have a question, you can't be afraid to ask! This is especially important when it comes to placing content you write for another blog on your own site. Discuss this with the blog before even posting your work on your site. While this might seem crazy (after all, it is *your* content), it is important to keep a good relationship with other blogs. Some blogs don't have a problem with this, while others do - make sure it is discussed before you make a mistake and are no longer asked back.

- **Give credit where credit is due.** If you quote, paraphrase, or use another site for inspiration, make sure you provide a link back to the author's page. The Internet is huge, but it's not that hard to find out if others are stealing your work. When in doubt, cite!

- **Make sure you get credit as well**. Provide the blog with a professional-looking picture and less than 500 character bio about you with links to your blog, Twitter account, and LinkedIn profile. If they use Twitter to blast their newest blog articles, request that they mention you when doing so. Remember that all blogs have a different way of setting up their blog formats, but if they are trying to pass off your work as their own without giving you credit, seriously consider the partnership you're entering into.

I use my blogs which are attached and fed through my LinkedIn and Twitter accounts and as a business they appear on my website at the bottom of the Home Page.

Tips when Blogging

- Use a platform that you are comfortable with, Blogger, Word press etc.;
- Content is more important than appearance;
- Stick to a topic or area;
- Make your blog helpful to readers;
- Opinion is fine but ensure your facts are correct;
- Post on a regular basis;
- Promote your blog on Face book, Twitter, LinkedIn etc.;
- Promote and link to other blogs and news websites;
- Use Mashable, Alltop etc. for ideas.

UNIT 23: BODY LANGUAGE

Body language can be defined as a form of non verbal communication, consisting of body pose, gestures, and eye movements. People often send and interpret such signals unconsciously.

The posh word for all this is Kinesics, but much more importantly it has a very powerful influence, which is often neither properly understood nor recognised.

Body language may provide clues as to the attitude or state of mind of a person. For instance, it may indicate aggression, attentiveness, nerves, boredom, pleasure, amusement and many other clues.

Lets fast forward until we reach that point which, hopefully, will be upon you all soon – the interview. You are about to complete the important <u>triangle.</u> You have issued your written communication in the form of a well thought through covering letter and a concise, punchy CV, setting out your attributes and skills in a manner which has been sufficiently impressive to cause your prospective employer to invite you for a first interview. Well done!!

You have been bright enough to really do your homework on the company concerned, not only by looking them up on the internet but by talking to friends, colleagues and associates and even making a call or two to the main number of the company and asking a few innocent questions – to which the uninitiated will almost always supply useful information – and you now stand at the door of the interview room. Incidentally, your interview starts as you enter the site of your prospective employer. You may be surprised to know that sometimes a call will be made to Reception or to a secretary to find out your attitude and behaviour prior to being brought to the formal interview room.

When you get in there you will find that the interviewer or interviewers will have a copy of your written CV in front of them. To be successful you need now to deploy TWO additional skills.

Firstly, and most obviously, you will be employing your verbal skills, not only in responding to questions from the interviewers but in formulating questions of your own. Interviewing techniques is a subject you will learn on through the process of reading this book.

But there is one more skill that is vitally important and which if ignored or not understood, will, without a shadow of doubt, torpedo your chances of getting the job: Kinesics or body language.

It has been shown by a number of eminent researchers that something in excess of 75% of human communication consists of body language and paralinguistic clues and only 25% by the verbal's. Body language is therefore a key factor and if you are being interviewed by the HR department it could very well be that the person opposite you has been trained to read and interpret the signs. It is less likely in the case of a line manager but even he will react instinctively to your signs and gestures.

Body language is not a tool to trap you and indeed it can be used by the interviewer to put you at your ease at the start of the interview.

Body language can come from the use of your eyes, your legs, your arms, your face, your head movements, your hands and from the invasion of personal space. Your tone of voice can also give clues to your interviewer. For example, in many cases, people's voices rise half an octave if they are telling less than the truth.

In the same way that with your CV you have to establish a rapport before the employer has read the first half page, so the first minutes of an interview, including your arrival and greeting, are vital. There will generally be an element of small talk to put you at your ease and your body language will stand out particularly at this stage.

Now I don't want you to think that you should think through a set of non verbal communications before you go in for interview and then try to deploy them during the course of the next half hour.

I have conducted interviews where the applicant has come rushing into the room with a gushing grin, shaken my hand violently and plonked himself down expectantly in the chair; equally I have had people come into the room with eyes looking down and half whispering a greeting. Obviously, you will avoid such extremes but you need to be aware of that area in the middle which can reveal to the interviewer more than you intended.

One of the most basic and powerful signals is when a person crosses his or her <u>arms</u> across the chest. This can indicate that a person is putting up an unconscious barrier and should be avoided at all costs, especially if the person is at the same time leaning away from the interviewer.

<u>Eyes</u> are another key area. Try to keep a consistent, friendly eye contact. This can indicate that you are thinking positively of what the interviewer is saying. An averted gaze can indicate boredom, disbelief or some other negative connotation.

<u>Hands</u> are a tricky area. They can be very useful appendages on many occasions but a distinct hindrance on others. Why do you think the Duke of Edinburgh is usually seen with his hands behind his back? It is to stop them getting in the way. Hands, unemployed and just hanging down or flapping about look awful. At interview, try keeping your hands on your knees or in your lap most of the time, making use of them as appropriate for emphasising any point you want to make.

<u>Legs</u> are best left uncrossed. A leg crossed away from the person being addressed can be seen as a 'keep off' sign or a sign of overconfidence.

Avoid <u>fidgeting.</u> Unintentional gestures like rubbing your face, scratching your nose, and touching your hair can break everybody's concentration.

If you have any <u>personal mannerisms</u>, do try to keep these in check. I have a friend who uses the Christian name of the person she is addressing at least once in every sentence. It is incredibly annoying. Equally avoid using words such as 'like' or 'yerknow' if you possibly can.

Keep your <u>mouth </u>closed, except when speaking. A slack jaw sends all the wrong sort of signals.

Finally, and very important when you are not sitting down, don't invade other people's space; don't invade the so-called <u>bubble zone</u>. There are four different zones of personal space. The first zone is called intimate distance and ranges from touching to 18 inches. This is strictly for lovers! The second is from 18 inches to four feet and this is for friends and associates. Except when you are actually shaking hands, try to keep at least four feet away, in the so-called social zone. The fourth zone, of over 8 feet, which is used for speeches, lectures etc. is not relevant to us today.

So, do your homework, exude confidence, be friendly, but not overfriendly, be positive and avoid annoying anyone with your body language.

Good luck with the interview. And, in the nicest possible sense we hope not to see you again!

UNIT 24: SOCIAL NETWORKING

THE SIX-STEP APPROACH: A NETWORKING STRATEGY

By approaching your networking in a professional and appropriate manner, you will benefit from one of the great truths of job hunting, best summed up by Richard Bolles in *What Color is your Parachute?*: "How you go about your job search says as much about you as your qualifications and experience".

The goal of your networking strategy is to gain information and contacts that will be valuable in your job search. In drawing up this strategy, you should be aware of the importance of second generation or referred contacts. Research carried out by London Business School has discovered that of those people who succeeded in getting a job through networking:

- 13% got their position through their contacts (1st generation)

- 70% got their position through their contacts' contacts (2nd generation)

- 17% got their position through those contacts' contacts (3rd generation).

Two important conclusions follow:

1. Never underestimate the contacts you have; their value lies in their own contacts, which may range wider than you think. The history of networking is littered with people who found their path to a new position through someone whose usefulness they had initially discounted. Actual examples include retired fathers-in-law who turn out to spend their spare time playing golf with the local captains of industry or next door neighbours with nephews puzzling over how to implement the major growth plans of their expanding companies.

2. One of the key questions to use with any contact is "Who else should I be speaking to in your organisation/profession/industry".

Step 1

Draw up your list of contacts: friends, colleagues, alumni and business contacts. At this stage make it as long as you like: the more the merrier, as it can be weeded later. This working document/spreadsheet should continually be updated and expanded.

Step 2

Clarify where you are in terms of your career direction. If you are clear about what kind of role you want next, excellent; if not then arrange some early meetings with your closest contacts, ideally people who know what you are like to work with.

One key aim of these early meetings will be to refine your direction pretty quickly, so while sounding out their opinion, make it clear to them that these are early musings rather than a thought through strategy. With these contacts you can even ask the question "What do *you* think I should do next?".

It is also useful to have a list of criteria gained from psychometrics and self-awareness exercises against which to evaluate suggestions.

Step 3

Categorise your contacts. There are many ways of classifying contacts; the most useful provide a framework for indentifying the most useful approach for each: our suggestion is that contacts fall into five categories in two classes:

Category:		Class:
1. MORALE BOOSTERS	}	SUPPORTERS
2. CRITICAL FRIENDS	}	
3. POTENTIAL EMPLOYERS	}	
4. GATEKEEPERS	}	ROUTE-FINDERS
5. NODES	}	

Looking at each in turn:

SUPPORTERS are close contacts and allies who know you well and want you to succeed. With them you can be open and frank about such things as your initial indecision on direction but they will hope and expect you to gain direction as your networking campaign progresses.

Morale Boosters are people you feel good with, who energise you by reaffirming your confidence and sense of self. They are great at providing support and encouragement when you go through a bad patch and at celebrating success when things go well.

Critical Friends can be relied on to provide honest, informed feedback and advice. They are the ones that will give you a clear appraisal of how you come over and will shake you out of your lethargy if that's what needs doing.

Naturally, supports can fall into both categories. Some can also fall into the second class of contact:

ROUTE-FINDERS who provide information and contacts that help to progress you through your network.

Potential Employers, as the name implies, can offer you a job and identifying them is a key goal of networking. Often they are the specific person you will work for in the new organisation but they can also be influential figures within it. Before contacting them directly, you will aim to be fully informed about them as well as their organisation, so that your approach is both professional and appropriate, including an element of cultural 'tuning'.

Gatekeepers can make your life easy or difficult in gaining access to Potential Employers and Nodes. They may be receptionists, a PA or the Head of HR.

Nodes are people whose working life brings them into contact with large numbers of your potential employers (see Figure 1). They can rapidly provide invaluable information on developments in this group as well as hard-to-assess clues on cultural match. Examples include industry or trade association employees, particularly those whose work brings them into contact with the membership. More specifically, if you are in sales, buyers can be useful contacts because they will deal with a wide range of sales representatives; similarly buyers should talk to salespeople or suppliers.

FIGURE 1

Potential Employers

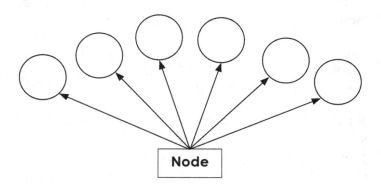

STEP 4

Become a valuable contact yourself. Attendance at upcoming conferences or exhibitions relevant to your target industry or job function is one way of getting a flying start in becoming a valuable source of information. Exhibitions can help you discover the latest product or service developments and tend to be free; as a minimum, the catalogue of exhibitors gets you an up-to-date address list. Conferences, though, can be expensive; if possible, attend on behalf of your company before you leave.

The more networking you do within your target industry, the more you will be able to develop your knowledge base and become a useful network contact for others, building your self-confidence through turning your network meetings into meetings of mutual interest, based on parity in the information exchange.

STEP 5

Just do it. Your task now is to create momentum in your job search. Of course making the phone calls and arranging meetings is hard work initially. You are overcoming the job searching inertia built up during years of gainful employment but the more you do it, the easier it becomes. Before you start, it is easy to imagine the whole process as likely to result in a series of negative and/or humiliating encounters. Once you get things moving, you will begin to have real, positive networking experiences, on which you can capitalise. Before each contact think through the checklist:

1. What do I want from this contact? Is the goal to obtain a meeting, some specific information or new contact? Or all three?

2. What do I have to offer the contact? (i.e. WIIFT – What's in it for them?)

3. What is the most appropriate medium: phone call, letter or email?

4. If I get through to their voicemail, what do I say?

5. Is there a fallback goal I can get, something that will be easy for them to grant and preserves the contact?

6. Remember to keep it professional and appropriate at all times, but not at the expense of humanity and humour.

Remember that your goal for a specific meeting will depend into which category the contact belongs:

Morale Boosters can be useful in just reintroducing a sense of the normal back into your life. If they are people with whom you played sport or met socially then maintaining the typical contact may be all that is required. Don't just use them as someone to moan to if you've had a bad couple of days; also let them know you value the continuity of your normal relationship (which may be a relief to them).

Critical friends come into their own when you feel you would like to review what's been happening. Their perspective may be useful in making sense of some of the frustrations of job search.

Gatekeepers can often be seen as barriers; your aim should be to turn them in to allies. Recognising that they have a role to play and finding ways for them to help you is one approach, e.g. by getting them to suggest a good time to call. If all else fails and you come across someone who really blocks everything you try, then try calling your target before 08:45 or after 18:00.

Nodes are key members of your network. Your aim is to tap into their contacts, so you need to come over as credible, which means time spent on preparation. Even if they genuinely have their finger on the pulse of what is going on in your target industry, they still might be interested in comparing notes with what you have gleaned from your networking. Typically they are most useful in (a) identifying potential employers and (b) providing hints on how/when to approach them.

Remember: Goalless = Clueless

Having obtained a meeting, it is a major error to waste this opportunity to go through things in depth by turning up goalless. A pleasant but aimless discussion does you no good and may inhibit further referrals from that person. Remember who you are and why you are there and start by focusing the discussion within it. The aim could be a general update on what is happening within the industry or specific information on one or two companies. Increasingly your questions should demonstrate your depth of knowledge and frequently you will find that you have become a useful source of information as well as a recipient.

As you get more informed, your goals are likely to be more specific; your purpose may get smaller. But remember at any stage it can be useful, possibly at the end of a discussion, to get your contact to think outside the box.

STEP 6

Capitalise on and Celebrate Success!

Be aware of your energy levels; any kind of success can generate positive energy which you should capitalise on e.g. by making that difficult/crucial phone call you have been putting off all day. So, to use a mixed metaphor:

Don't rest on your laurels: ride the wave!

Just as importantly, once you have successfully landed your new job, let your contacts know and thank them for their assistance. A celebratory letter/email/drink/meal could set the seal on a long term and mutually valuable network ally.

Attend to Impress – First and Last Contact

Be selective on what you attend and look at it as a Strategy:

- Dress to impress – wear suitable clothes;

- Research the network;

- Have your business cards to hand;

- Have a strategy in mind – who do you want to make contact with?

- Cost and location – plan;

- Do not arrive too early or late;

- Sign in and collect list of attendees or request beforehand;

- Smile and be ready to shake hands and give a polite introduction;

- Approach enthusiastically – "Hello I am...." ;

- Do not barge into conversations;

- Listen – show an interest in the people there;

- This is not a selling exercise – but an engagement opportunity;
- Think: What is your purpose?
- Have an introduction ready!
- Work the room.

DO NOT:

- Barge into conversations;
- Stand there without speaking – make your introduction – timing!
- Do not go unprepared with a Business Card or strap line;
- I am Joe Smith and I am here today to engage and make contacts as I am looking for opportunities within the Engineering Sector, as I am a Civil Engineer with 20 years' experience - AND THEN NOT ASK WHAT THEY DO?

FOLLOW UP

- Move around the room and nail the introductions you want;
- Follow up with email/call;
- Always show an interest in others;
- Observe the style;
- Remember your BODY LANGUAGE;
- Keep to your PLAN;

- Why are you there?

- Who do you want to meet?

- Seek new opportunities;

- Impress and make an impact;

- Can they introduce you to someone you need?

- Be careful of SELLING and do not oversell!

- Mirror the style of the Network and fit in;

- Enjoy but it is not a night out!

UNIT 25: TRANSFERABLE SKILLS

Transferable Skills

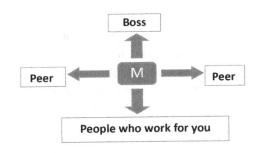

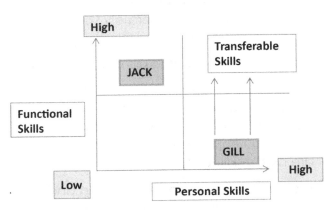

TRANSFERABLE SKILLS – Exercise One

Complete a separate worksheet for each job or activity.

For this exercise take your last three Jobs and three Activities – could be Voluntary, Board Membership or other.

1. In the Tasks column list each function of your job or activity;

2. Then in the Skills column list the skill you use or used to complete the corresponding task. Below are some examples of transferable skills. Do not limit yourself to the ones listed;

3. In the Skill Level column rate yourself according to your level of competency (1=highly skilled; 2=moderately skilled; 3=needs improvement);

4. Place a * next to those skills which you enjoy using;

5. After you have completed all worksheets, write a list of those skills which you enjoy using and in which you are highly skilled [1];

6. Then list those skills you enjoy using and in which you are moderately skilled [2];

7. You can also keep a separate list of those skills in which you need improvement [3] but enjoy using. Set

that list aside. These skills need to be added to your Personal Career Development Plan which is a tool to use when JOB SEARCHING and within your new role to support and enable your success for immediate action.

My Skills		
Job or Activity		
Tasks	Skills	Skill Level

- Plan and arrange events and activities
- Delegate responsibility
- Motivate others
- Attend to visual detail
- Assess and evaluate my own work
- Assess and evaluate others' work
- Deal with obstacles and crises
- Multi-task
- Present written material
- Present material orally
- Manage time
- Repair equipment or machinery
- Keep records
- Handle complaints
- Coordinate fundraising activities
- Coaching/Mentoring

- Research build or construct
- Design buildings, furniture, etc.
- Manage finances
- Speak a foreign language (specify language)
- Use sign language
- Utilise computer software (specify programmes)
- Train or teach others
- Identify and manage ethical issues.

Now produce from the exercise above:

1. Skills that you like doing and are good at;

2. Skills that you are moderately good at and are okay with;

3. Skills that you need to improve and are not so keen on.

Create TABLE ONE - that will give you areas of work you could NOW move into.

CREATE TABLE TWO

Will give you areas of work you could with a little polish move into.

TABLE THREE

Will give you areas of work you could only move into by taking ACTION in your PCDP.

- Note: This exercise will support your CV – Profiles – Group Dynamics and working in a Team – Interview Techniques for you to move forward. This Unit will give you the opportunity to focus on your CORE SKILLS to compliment your FUNCTIONAL SKILLS.

UNIT 26: COMMUNICATION SKILLS

REFLECTION ANDREINVENTION

The way to self confidence is Reinvention

For those of us who have been made redundant or face redundancy, this is a 'true awakening' as we think we know ourselves! Being made redundant is not to be taken personally and it is the role you have been in that is redundant not YOU! In order to move on with these Units – you have to let go of the Past and Reclaim a Future!

It is surprising how differently we see ourselves compared to how other people see us. Our friends and relatives may see us as strong, intelligent people, but sometimes in our work, we lose ourselves – we get used to acting out a role and neglect who we truly are. We can then become trapped within a role which is not what we are comfortable with.

Making changes

Psychologist Timothy Butler in his book '*Getting Unstuck*'" states that this is a **psychological impasse being stuck or paralysed.** You may now be desperate to change in order to find work and the best way out of '**impasse**' is to r**einvent yourself!**

Celebrities who have reinvented themselves:

- Madonna
- David Beckham
- Catherine Zeta-Jones
- Politicians and entrepreneurs and many more.

UNIT 27: REINVENTION

Exercise - Reinvention

Write a list of all the people you know who have reinvented themselves.

This is not a PR gimmick– if you do not write your list you cannot move on in your life and you are limiting yourself. If celebrities can do it – **so can you!** – stay relevant to your audience of work.

In this part, we cover some basic principles about reflection. These principles

represent the best practices for reflection as part of service and service-learning. They can be presented as the 4 Cs:

Continuous

- Reflection should be an ongoing part of the service performed;

- This allows participants to continue seeing the world in new ways;

- This fosters a commitment to long-term reflective action and a growing awareness that may lead to more complex service, activism, and social change efforts.

Connected

- Reflection should be connected to the other quality components: orientation, training and education;

- Used to illustrate (connect) theories to real life;

- Fosters more effective service and more effective learning.

Challenging

Individuals ask and answer questions or statements which may be unfamiliar or uncomfortable:

- This forces participants to think in new ways and question their perceptions of events and issues.

Contextualized

- Reflection is a purposeful way to connect thought and action;

- Reflection activities should be appropriate for the setting (level of formality).

Interactive piece

Have you thought now about your own service work, activism, or service learning and whether the reflection they are doing meets these 4 Cs. Now generate ideas of ways that reflection can be conducted to meet the 4Cs. Have you shared this within your Peer Groups?

UNIT 28: REFLECTION

Facilitation Rules for Reflection

First, review the cooperative learning roles:

Cooperative learning has many different roles for team members during group activities. Suggestion: in groups of four, one person should take both the timekeeper and observer role. In groups of three, another person should take both the recorder and reporter roles. Make sure to assume a different role each time you work in a cooperative learning group. Group members should take turns, so everyone gets a chance to experience each role.

- **Facilitator** - the person responsible for organising the reflection and work of the group, and being sure the group stays on task.

- **Recorder** - the person who takes notes, writes on newsprint as the group brainstorms, and/or prepares the newsprint.

- **Reporter** - the person who shares with other teams the work or conclusions of the team.

- **Timekeeper -** the person who assures that the team is able to devote appropriate time to each element of reflection/assigned task and complete all its tasks within the allotted time; this role is especially useful when the team has a tight deadline.

- **Observer-** the person who watches the interaction of the group members and report son difficulties or successes in group interaction.

Then, present some DON'Ts for facilitating reflection (and in general),asking people why they think these tips make sense (or don't if they disagree):

- Downplaying people's ideas;

- Pushing personal agendas and opinions as the 'right' answer or opinion about inexperience;

- Dominating the group or doing all the talking;

- Saying "umm", "aahh" etc.;

- Reading from a manuscript;

- Telling inappropriate or offensive stories;

- Allowing people to bully others in the group into adopting their point of view;

- Taking a stance with one section of the group;

- Telling too much about your personal experiences and life: keep a healthy balance- you are seen as the leader in the room;
- Assuming the demographics, opinions, or perspectives of your group.

Then, present these basic tips:

- Establish Group Norms (such as with the roles);
- Watch the time;
- Validate everyone's opinions;
- Be challenging;
- Be neutral.

Finally, explain some examples of ways that facilitation tools can be used to move through various parts of the cycle or model.

You could model one or more, depending on time, and identifying a single sample focus:

Yarn Toss: Use a ball of yarn that is passed as people 'weave a web' of their reflections;

Post-Its: Have people post questions they encounter in their minds as they process observations; then sort through and group questions, and use them for discussion;

Ball Game: Use a ball or token to move discussion around, combining with provocative Questions.

UNIT 29: BRANDING

Finding the real you – BRANDING

This normally starts with your **appearance** – this is your branding! This should be a reflection of inner self and requires action. Clearing out your wardrobe is a start.

Branding – The Real Me

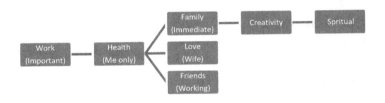

Branding – The Changed Me To be continued !

What I consider my:

Strengths	Weaknesses
Good communicator	Impatient - has to be done now
IT skills	Do the work rather than delegate – it's quicker
Creative	Always think I'm right
Good engineering knowledge	Sometimes come across as negative
Goods sales knowledge	Say what I think – don't hold back?
Excellent time keeping	Take on too much/ volunteer too much
Organised	Sometimes jump the gun
Motivated by work	Sometimes a little shy
Can work under pressure	Written skills
Enthusiastic	
Innovative	
Hard worker	
Team player	
Forward thinker	
Multi skilled	
Flexible	
Passion to do a job well	
Determined	
Reliable / Good time keeper	
Conscientious	

My 12 month ACTION plan

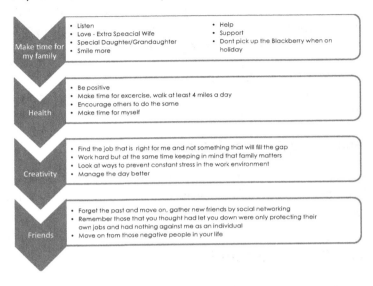

Make time for my family	• Listen • Love - Extra Speacial Wife • Special Daughter/Grandaughter • Smile more	• Help • Support • Dont pick up the Blackberry when on holiday
Health	• Be positive • Make time for excercise, walk at least 4 miles a day • Encourage others to do the same • Make time for myself	
Creativity	• Find the job that is right for me and not something that will fill the gap • Work hard but at the same time keeping in mind that family matters • Look at ways to prevent constant stress in the work environment • Manage the day better	
Friends	• Forget the past and move on, gather new friends by social networking • Remember those that you thought had let you down were only protecting their own jobs and had nothing against me as an individual • Move on from those negative people in your life	

You must have a clear understanding of who you are to do this exercise.

Exercise Two

Write a list of the following headings and descriptive words related to how you feel about each one:

Work   Family   Health   Love   Friends
Creativity   Spirituality

Now take a look at the words- are you proud, frustrated or surprised at any of the words that define you?

I used to define myself as Work being the number one Priority and now, 20 years later, I put Health as my number one Priority. This is because upon Reflection when I was very ill and supported a parent who was ill, this made me realise that without your Health you cannot enjoy any of the other values.

I have also noted that over the last 20 years of delivering this exercise, the shift has moved from Work to Family.

Author of your own biography

Dr David Lewis in his book *'The Mind Lab'*, defines that reinvention is that **you** are the author of your own biography.

ADDITIONAL EXERCISES

1. Write down the three main choices you made in your life – did you make them or did someone, or something, play a major role in this? For example: going to University? Were you in control at that time? Was it a **positive/negative** impact?

2. If you had made some different choices would your life be different now?

That is the SELF you left behind. How do you feel about that Self?

3. Are you relieved or do you envy the person you left behind?

4. Write down the top ten things that you aim to achieve this year.

5. What is your purpose in life?

Now – base the above exercise on your future decisions to help you make the right decisions.

My Purpose for 2013 is to LEARN – LIVE AND LOVE!

Know Yourself – the Employee

What have you done in the last 12 months which you are proud of?

Now, imagine one year from now what you could achieve and that you feel you would be proud of?

Is this a **contribution t**o your life?

Know your Audience – the Employer

People that have an effect on the decisions we make are called 'stakeholders' and it does not mean they always work in our favour or interest. You must stay in control and imagine how they see your strengths/weaknesses (areas for development);if they do not have vision they are unable to see you for your strengths but they do see you for their own game.

UNIT 30: UNIQUE SELLING POINT

What is your USP? You have to discover this and promote this in all your verbal and non verbal communications:

'Lower price' based USP options include...

Lowest price does not guarantee that it is the best value for money for employers and it is not the way to present yourself. Value yourself and research what you are worth in your industry but be realistic. Can you look at your budget and decide on the minimum you could accept to start with, to be reassessed later on – say after your 6 month probation period.

'Service' based USP options include...

Do you promote the best value re: 'delivery of service'?

'Convenience' based USP options include...

Do you live nearer the site than your competitors or are you willing, flexible and able to travel to one or many sites?

'Choice' based USP options include...

- Choice regarding pricing levels. Do you offer the Employer the 'best value for their money' and are you an investment?
- Choice regarding expertise sought;
- Choice regarding length of programme or arrangement;
- Choice regarding stages or modules adopted;
- Choice regarding various solutions offered;
- Choice regarding person to deal with;
- Choice regarding frequency of programme or arrangement;
- Choice regarding method of delivery of your service.

'Guarantee' based USP options include...

- What Guarantees can you bring to the table to reassure the Employer?
- Most wide ranging guarantee in the market place;
- Guarantee a specific performance or result;
- Guarantee a specific level of satisfaction;
- Guarantee a specific level of service from you.

'Innovation' based USP options include...

- Employers now look for an Entrepreneurial 'Mind Set' – do you have that?
- Most fashionable;
- New approach, technique, methodology, process or combination;
- Innovative methods;
- Clever or unusual presentation;
- Unique delivery of service.

'Technology' based USP options include...

New technological knowledge.

'Speed' based USP options include...

Promise a specific performance in terms of time... Guaranteed!

'Quality' based USP options include...

- Detail the number of quality checks or steps and the procedures involved;
- Paint a word picture of how you conduct your business in a quality fashion;
- Detail the standards you expect and uphold;

- Detail your methods for choosing employees, materials, and other key quality ingredients;

- Detail the training you and your team members undergo before being allowed to conduct business or deal with customers;

- Explain how slowly/carefully you do things and why.

'Exclusivity' based USP options include...

- You are the EXCLUSIVE OFFER;

- Does the Employer measure up?

- Must be prepared to wait – working notice;

- Only available to best customers, clients or patients;

- Must be referred by one of our customers, clients or patients.

'Tradition' based USP options include...

Can the Employer trust your integrity that you have had over 20 years at a senior level in their industry?

'Niche' based USP options include...

- Specialise in a particular field of interest;

- Specialise in a particular product or service;

- Specialise in a particular area or region;

- Specialise in a particular type of customer;

- Become the expert spokesman for your chosen niche by publishing your views.

'Information' based USP options include...

You can offer to do a week as a Placement to see how you both fit in with each other – a free sample of your skills.

'Solution' based USP options include...

- Offering an easier way to achieve any of the human emotional needs;

- Offering a unique solution to a problem;

- Showing people how you have uniquely addressed their fears or frustrations;

- Using 'specificity' can help build uniqueness into your message;

- Proprietary words and phrases can also help build uniqueness into the service you provide.

'Culture' based USP options include...

- Communicate your beliefs and the specific standards you expect of yourself;

- Communicate your beliefs and the specific standards you expect of your customers, clients or patients;

- Communicate your beliefs and the specific standards you expect of others.

Testimonial Based USP options include ...

- References;

- Testimonials on LinkedIn Profile;

- Word of mouth as a recommendation from present employers or other organisations or competitors.

'Sensory' based USP options include...

Using two of the five senses – SIGHT (presentation) and SOUND (pitch of voice).

UNIT 31: SELF CONFIDENCE AND CONFIDENCE BUILDING

From the quietly confident doctor whose advice we rely on, to the charismatic confidence of an inspiring speaker, self-confident people have qualities that everyone admires.

Self-confidence is extremely important in almost every aspect of our lives, yet so many people struggle to find it. Sadly, this can be a vicious circle: people who lack self-confidence can find it difficult to become successful.

After all, most people are reluctant to back a project that is being pitched by someone who is nervous, fumbling and overly apologetic.

On the other hand, you might be persuaded by someone who speaks clearly, who holds his or her head high, who answers questions assuredly, and who readily admits when he or she does not know something.

Self-confident people inspire confidence in others: their audience, their peers, their bosses, their customers, and their friends. Gaining the confidence of others is one of the key ways in which a self-confident person finds success.

The good news is that self-confidence really can be learned and built on. And, whether you're working on your own self-confidence or building the confidence of people around you, it's well-worth the effort!

How Confident do You Seem to Others?

Your level of self-confidence can show in many ways: your behaviour, your body language, how you speak, what you say, and so on. Look at the following comparisons of common confident behaviour with behaviour associated with low self-confidence. Which thoughts or actions do you recognise in yourself and people around you?

Self-Confident	Low Self-Confidence
Doing what you believe to be right, even if others mock or criticise you for it.	Governing your behaviour based on what other people think.
Being willing to take risks and go the extra mile to achieve better things.	Staying in your comfort zone, fearing failure and so avoid taking risks.
Admitting your mistakes, and learning from them.	Working hard to cover up mistakes, and hoping that you can fix the problem before anyone notices.

Waiting for others to congratulate you on your accomplishments.	Extolling your own virtues as often as possible to as many people as possible.
Accepting compliments graciously: "Thanks, I really worked hard on that prospectus. I'm pleased you recognise my efforts."	Dismissing compliments offhandedly: "Oh that prospectus was nothing really, anyone could have done it."

As you can see from these examples, low self-confidence can be self-destructive, and it often manifests itself as negativity. Self-confident people are generally more positive – they believe in themselves and their abilities, and they also believe in living life to the full.

What is Self-Confidence?

Two main things contribute to self-confidence: self-efficacy and self-esteem.

We gain a sense of **self-efficacy** when we see ourselves (and others similar to ourselves) mastering skills and achieving goals that matter in those skill areas. This is the confidence that, if we learn and work hard in a particular area, we'll succeed; and it's this type of confidence that leads people to accept difficult challenges and persist in the face of setbacks.

This overlaps with the idea of **self-esteem**, which is a more general sense that we can cope with what's going on in our lives and that we have a right to be happy. Partly, this comes from a feeling that the people around us approve of us, which we may or may not be able to control. However, it also comes from the sense that we are behaving virtuously, that we're competent at what we do, and that we can compete successfully when we put our minds to it.

Some people believe that self-confidence can be built with affirmations and positive thinking. We believe that there's some truth in this, but that it's just as important to build self-confidence by setting and achieving goals – thereby **building competence**. Without this underlying competence, you don't have self-confidence: you have shallow over-confidence, with all of the issues, upset and failure that this brings.

Building Self-Confidence

So how do you build this sense of balanced self-confidence, founded on a firm appreciation of reality?

The bad news is that there's no quick fix, or five-minute solution.

The good news is that building self-confidence is readily achievable, just as long as you have the focus and determination to carry things through. And what's even better is that the things you'll do to build self-confidence will also build success

– after all, your confidence will come from real, solid achievement. No-one can take this away from you!

So here are our three steps to self-confidence, for which we'll use the metaphor of a journey: preparing for your journey; setting out; and accelerating towards success.

STEP 1: Preparing for Your Journey

The first step involves getting yourself ready for your journey to self-confidence. You need to take stock of where you are, think about where you want to go, get yourself in the right mindset for your journey, and commit yourself to starting it and staying with it.

In preparing for your journey, do these five things:

Look at what you've already achieved

Think about your life so far, and list the ten best things you've achieved in an 'Achievement Log'. Perhaps you came top in an important test or exam, played a key role in an important team, produced the best sales figures in a period, did something that made a key difference in someone else's life, or delivered a project that meant a lot for your business.

Put these into a smartly formatted document, which you can look at often. And then spend a few minutes each week enjoying the success you've already had!

Think about your strengths

Make sure that you enjoy a few minutes reflecting on your strengths.

Think about what's important to you, and where you want to go

Next, think about the things that are really important to you, and what you want to achieve with your life.

Setting goals

Having set the major goals in your life, identify the first step in each. Make sure it's a very small step, perhaps taking no more than an hour to complete.

Start managing your mind

Create strong mental images of yourself in that new job role.

And then commit yourself to success!

The final part of preparing for the journey is to make a clear and unequivocal promise to yourself that you are absolutely committed to your journey, and that you will do all in your power to achieve it.

If, as you're doing it, you find doubts starting to surface, write them down and challenge them calmly and rationally. If they dissolve under scrutiny, that's great. However, if they are based on genuine risks, make sure you set additional goals to manage these appropriately.

Either way, make that promise!

Tip:

Self-confidence is about balance. At one extreme, we have people with low self-confidence. At the other end, we have people who may be over-confident.

If you are under-confident, you'll avoid taking risks and stretching yourself, and you might not try at all. And if you're over-confident, you may take on too much risk, stretch yourself beyond your capabilities, and crash badly. You may also find that you're so optimistic that you don't try hard enough to truly succeed.

Getting this right is a matter of having the right amount of confidence, founded in reality and on your true ability. With the right amount of self-confidence, you will take informed risks, stretch yourself (but not beyond your abilities) and try hard.

STEP 2: Setting Out

This is where you start, ever so slowly, moving towards your goal. By doing the right things, and starting with small, easy wins, you'll put yourself on the path to success – and start building the self-confidence that comes with this.

Build the knowledge you need to succeed

Looking at your goals, identify the skills you'll need to achieve them and then look at how you can acquire these skills confidently and well. Don't just accept a sketchy, just-good-enough solution – look for a solution, a programme or a course that fully equips you to achieve what you want to achieve and, ideally, gives you a certificate or qualification you can be proud of.

Focus on the basics

When you're starting, don't try to do anything clever or elaborate. And don't reach for perfection – just enjoy doing simple things successfully and well.

Set small goals, and achieve them

Starting with the very small goals you identified in Step 1, get in the habit of setting them, achieving them, and celebrating that achievement. Don't make goals particularly challenging at this stage, just get into the habit of achieving them and celebrating them. And, little by little, start piling up the successes!

Keep managing your mind

Stay on top of that positive thinking, keep celebrating and enjoying success, and keep those mental images strong.

And on the other side, learn to handle failure. Accept that mistakes happen when you're trying something new. In fact, if you get into the habit of treating mistakes as learning experiences, you can (almost) start to see them in a positive light. After all, there's a lot to be said for the saying, if it doesn't kill you, it makes you stronger,!

STEP3: Accelerating Towards Success

By this stage, you'll feel your self-confidence building. You'll have completed some of the courses you started in Step 2, and you'll have plenty of success to celebrate.

This is the time to start stretching yourself. Make the goals a bit bigger and the challenges a bit tougher. Increase the size of your commitment, and extend the skills you've proven into new, but closely related areas.

Tip 1:

Keep yourself grounded – this is where people tend to get over-confident and over-stretch themselves. And make sure you don't start enjoying cleverness for its own sake…

Tip 2:

Stretch yourself.

As long as you keep on stretching yourself enough, but not too much, you'll find your self-confidence building apace. What's more, you'll have earned your self-confidence – because you'll have put in the hard graft necessary to be successful.

Goal setting is arguably the most important skill you can learn to improve your self-confidence.

Key Points

Self-confidence is extremely important in almost every aspect of our lives, and people who lack it can find it difficult to become successful.

Two main things contribute to self-confidence: self-efficacy and self-esteem. You can develop self-confidence with these three steps:

1. Prepare for your journey.

2. Set out on your journey.

3. Accelerate towards success.

Goal setting is probably the most important activity that you can learn in order to improve your self-confidence.

UNIT 32: GOLDEN 'GEMS' OF ACHIEVING LIFE BALANCE

1: Maximum Performance

Lesson1 :Unlocking Your Potential

- Why you often perform below your capabilities

- How to lift the ceiling on your performance

- How to change your self-talk from negative to positive

- How to make your self-esteem go up overnight

- How to increase your income 25%-50% a year for the rest of your life.

Lesson 2 :Taking Charge of Your Life

- The true mark of maturity

- The one thing you must never give up

- How to eliminate (not stifle) all anger

- What to say to yourself when you feel negative

- What to say to others when they feel negative
- How to purge yourself of unhappy memories.

Lesson 3 :Seven Mental Laws

- How to unlock your capacity for high achievement
- How to accomplish more in two or three years than the average person does in a lifetime
- Seven mental laws you must stay in harmony with.

Lesson 4 :Using Your Subconscious Mind

- How to speak to your subconscious mind
- How to listen to your subconscious mind
- Exercises to be empowered by your subconscious mind.

2: Personal Strategic Planning

Lesson 5 :Strategic Thinking

- How to double or triple the speed you reach your goals
- The fate of not setting goals
- The most important mental skill you can develop

- The two games of success-inner and outer
- 'Blue sky' goals-why you should use them.

Lesson 6 :The Master Skill of Success

- How to override your failure mechanism
- How to trigger your success mechanism
- The price of success, and when you must pay it
- Seven obstacles to setting goals
- Five principles of goal setting
- Seven questions you must ask when setting goals.

Lesson 7 :Achieving Your Goals

- Now list 12 ESSENTIAL STEPS TO ACHIEVING YOUR GOALS - starting with
- Short term - medium term and long term goals - example:

Attend a Program to give me the tools to equip me with my JOB SEARCH - short term

Be in the JOB I deserve - medium term

Working on my PERSONAL CAREER DEVELOPMENT PLAN to achieve Promotion within the year - long term

Lesson 8 : Your Super conscious Mind

- How to produce a lot of work in a little time
- What '**Flow**' is-how to experience it
- An exercise to access your super conscious mind.

3: Managing Your Time

Lesson 9 : Mastering Your Time

- The core skill to all achievement
- How to get a 500% return on your investment of time
- The science of making lists
- A simple formula for getting organised
- How to use deadlines positively
- How to set priorities.

Lesson 10 : Maximizing Your Productivity

- The simple foundation of good work habits
- Four steps to high productivity
- Six steps to improving concentration
- How to overcome procrastination
- How to maintain a fast working tempo.

Lesson 11 :Streamlining Your Life

- Role of relationships in success
- How to take hold by letting go
- How to use zero-based thinking on everything
- When short-term pain means long-term gain.

Lesson 12 :Balancing Work and Family

- How to decide what's most important
- How relationships make 85% of your success
- When not to compromise
- How to design your ideal life style
- The balance between high tech and high touch
- When to delay commitments.

4: Career Advancement Strategies

Lesson 13 :Your Most Valuable Asset

- Being self-employed as a state of mind
- How to recognise and avoid time wasters
- Four steps to reading faster and more effectively
- How to increase your income ten times.

Lesson 14 :How to Get the Job You Want

- How to get the job you want
- How to find the best job for you
- Ways to assess your skills, abilities and interests
- How to write resumes that generate interviews
- How to find the right company
- Finding the right boss.

Lesson 15 :Leveraging Your Potential

- How to network and expand your contacts
- When you must buy your freedom
- How to achieve a successful image.

Lesson 16 :Fast Tracking Your Career

- How to fast-track your career
- How to move up faster
- How to change jobs or change companies
- How to develop your own power base
- Five keys to career advancement
- When you should be an opportunist
- How to avoid the salary ceiling.

5: Creating Wealth

Lesson 17 :Money and You

- Why anyone can get rich
- How you can still get rich in this 20th century? Five ways to become a millionaire
- How the wealthy preserve their capital
- How to ask your way to success.

Lesson 18 :The Way the World Works

- Why people succeed - why people fail
- When laziness and greed are good
- How to make impatience work for you
- Using selfishness constructively.

Lesson 19 :Blueprint for Financial Independence

- The mindset that leads to wealth
- How to be a magnet for money
- How to resist Parkinson's Law
- The three legs of financial planning
- Insurance - what's enough, what's too much.

Lesson 20 :Leadership - The Critical Difference

- Why you need a sense of mission

- How to use role models
- What books should a leader read
- How to be a role model.

6: Unlocking Your Mental Powers

Lesson 21 :The Psychology of Success

- How to be an 'inverse paranoid'
- The mindset of successful people
- How to form success habits
- Seven keys to mental fitness.

Lesson 22 :Stepping on Your Mental Accelerator

- How to unlock your potential with autogenic conditioning
- How to programme your subconscious mind
- How to reach the Alpha state
- How to use music for rapid learning.

Lesson 23 :Creative Problem Solving

- Your creativity and your IQ
- Why you are probably a genius
- How to learn to be creative
- Back from the future thinking
- How to come up with 250 new ideas a year.

Lesson 24 :Effective Decision Making

- How to test your assumptions
- How to evaluate your ideas
- How to sell your ideas to others.

7: Negotiating, Communicating, Persuading

Lesson 25 :Negotiation Strategies & Tactics, I

- How to get the best deal every time
- Is everything negotiable?
- The six styles of negotiating
- How to get a better price immediately.

Lesson 26 :Negotiation Strategies & Tactics, II

- The 'walk-away' method of negotiation
- How to negotiate with your boss for a raise
- How to prepare for negotiations
- How to give and get concessions.

Lesson 27 :Communicating for Results

- How you communicate what you are
- How to avoid message overload
- How to listen well
- How to listen empathetically.

Lesson 28 :How to Influence and Persuade Others

- How to earn cooperation
- Are you people-oriented or task-oriented?
- How to make a good first impression
- Getting people to return a favour
- Best time to ask for a favour.

8: Developing Your Character

Lesson 29 :The Development of Character

- Do you have a good reputation with yourself?
- How to prioritize your personal values.

Lesson 30 :The Power of Love

- The opposite of fear is not courage
- How to analyse your own fears
- Powerful techniques to overcome fear
- How to control your ego.

Lesson 31 :The Conquest of Fear

- Vince Lombardi's success secret
- The three measures of your willpower
- Napoleon Hill's great discovery

- Success wisdom from Confucius to Churchill to Coolidge
- How Conrad Hilton got rich.

Lesson 32 :The Iron Quality of Success

- How love dissolves fear
- How to act your way into loving
- How to become a totally loving person.

9: Your Energy and Dynamism

Lesson 33 :High Energy Performance, I

- How to achieve high levels of health and energy
- How to diet for high energy
- How to detoxify your body
- How to think thin
- How to live lean and mean.

Lesson 34 :High Energy Performance, II

- Seven healthy habits for living to 100
- Can you change your taste buds?
- How negative emotions wear you out
- Should you take vitamins and minerals?

Lesson 35 : Managing Stress and Achieving Personal Effectiveness, I

- How to be your own 'shrink'
- The one requisite for happiness and stress-free living
- How to strengthen your own immune system
- How you create your own stress.

Lesson 36 : Managing Stress and Achieving Personal Effectiveness, II

- Start using this 'worry buster'
- How to conquer the fear of failure
- The danger of incomplete transactions
- How to practice reality therapy.

10: Your Power with People

Lesson 37 : Developing a Success Personality, I

- The true source of all happiness
- The secret of impressing people
- How to raise other people's self-esteem
- Growth through forgiving others.

Lesson 38 : Developing a Success Personality, II

- Should you smile when you don't feel like it?

- Build trust through listening
- Advanced listening skills
- How to be an expert conversationalist.

Lesson 39 :Love and Romance

- How to stay in love
- What self-esteem does for your love life
- Your home life as a key to success
- How to rekindle love
- Six keys to success in relationships
- Six major problems in relationships.

Lesson 40 :How to Raise Super Kids

- Parenting styles that produce high achievers
- The effects of love deprivation
- How to help kids fulfil their potentials
- How to build children's self-esteem
- Four ways to convince your kids you love them.

11: Strategies for Business Success

Lesson 41 :Starting Your Own Business

- Should you consider entrepreneurship?
- The turning point that suggests starting a business

- The 'corridor principle' - key to success in life
- How to fight Murphy's Law
- New business traps to avoid
- Do's and don'ts of buying a business
- Is a franchise for you?

Lesson 42 :Marketing Strategy & Tactics

- How to test your new-business ideas
- How to make your product or service stand out
- The key purpose of any business (don't overlook it).

Lesson 43 :Getting the Money You Need

- How to start a business with little or no money
- How to use credit cards to start a business
- Why partnerships don't work
- How to select your business banker
- How to build an excellent credit history.

Lesson 44 :How to Sell Well

- How to get free advertising
- How to get on talk shows... and what to say

- How to create a company name, letterhead, etc.
- Twenty-one different ways to sell your product or service.

12: Building Your Estate

Lesson 45 :Real Estate Investment Strategies, I

- Financial independence from owning property
- The true way real estate is valued
- How to invest time when you have little money
- Why you must avoid the 'greater fool theory'.

Lesson 46 :Real Estate Investment Strategies, II

- How to increase property value by factor of 10 to 1
- The growth pattern of cities
- How to make an offer on property.

Lesson 47 :Managing For Results

- How to leverage your interactions with others
- The magic of systems

- How to get things done without doing them
- How to pick your business team
- Secrets of managing, delegating and supervising
- The trap of upward delegation.

Lesson 48 : How to Succeed by Really Trying

- How to develop a business plan for your life
- Why you should act as if you own the place
- Think rich - develop a prosperity consciousness
- How to concentrate your powers for maximum results
- Seven principles for constructive thinking
- Why there's always room at the top.

Exercise

Put these in order - PRIORITY at the beginning of the programme and again at the end. So how far you have travelled and have you changed?

WORK/CAREER   FAMILY/FRIENDS

MONEY / £Wealth   HEALTH/WELL BEING

CREATIVITY /INNOVATION SPIRITUALITY/INNER SPACE

I used to put WORK first, followed by money and wealth and then up until 2012 put Family and Friends at the top. Then when I was taken ill over Christmas 2012, I realised that without my health I could not enjoy any of the other areas of LIFE BALANCE - so for me it is HEALTH first for 2013!

UNIT 33: POSITIVE THINKING

Protect yourself from negative emotional contagion and develop a positive new outlook. We need to be able to lift ourselves out of a Triple Dip Recession and focus on a brighter and bigger future for ourselves and our family.

There is a financial crisis. We must not panic and, even though our concerns are valid, we don't want to become mob handed or indeed invest in the drama that is surrounding us at present.

Conversation

It is hard at present to avoid having a conversation which does not revolve around the above, though research suggests that this is neither healthy nor beneficial. If you collectively discuss the crisis then there is the possibility you will become depressed and anxiety will set in. So concentrate on the job around you, laugh with friends and family and if you are happy everyone around you becomes happy – it's infectious! The rush of the **'feel good'** factor is something to be shared and this **'karma'** then brushes off onto others.

Take out the feelings of cynicism and replace them with feelings of hope, love and optimism. Human beings need inspiration from self or others and this works positively within the dynamics of the group.

Elevation evokes us to lead a more positive life and the above gives us the desire to do so.

Reset Button

Robert Biswas-Diener, Author of 'Happiness - Positive Psychology' focuses on things that being unemployed cannot take away from you:

- positive thoughts
- strengths
- loyalty
- positivity
- happiness
- kindness
- motivation.

These traits will help us thrive in this economic downturn.

Identify with your strengths and stay focused on these and you will leave your depression behind you and will be happier. I cannot stress enough: spend any spare cash on an experience – go and listen to a guest speaker, attend an event, social networking, courses etc. - not another coffee in your favourite coffee shop!

Laughing

Laughing is contagious and as the saying goes 'when you laugh, the whole world laughs with you'. When we laugh we remain positive and send out positive signals to pick up 'good will'. When you are low and negative you will send out negative signals because your mind is rigid.

- Open up your mind
- Ease up
- Relax
- Accept yourself.

See Dr Michael Sinclair – Director of CITY Psychology Group

Ways to be positive:

1. Stop complaining and listening to complaints – only give positive criticism;

2. Read only success stories – people doing well in their career, sport, business etc;

3. Join a group – we become more competitive and need the support of others – network!

4. Share resources - by pooling your skills and sharing these, this builds networks and enhances your strengths;

5. Volunteer – support a group within your community, one you are inspired by;

6. Explore – explore – explore!

7. Be adventurous – try new things- this generates positive thoughts. Meeting new people will BOOST YOUR POSITIVE ENERGY!

8. Join a gym – take the opportunity of a free week's trial. A well tuned body is a well tuned mind;

9. Create new contacts, new topics and new OPPORTUNITIES!

NOW – here is your challenge!

Let us cascade our happiness to our friends and family and be daring and start conversations which are POSITIVE!

Exercise

Write a list of how <u>not</u> to start a conversation (negative conversation)

Example: "What awful weather we are having again."

Write a list on how to start a <u>positive</u> conversation.

Example: "What a glorious day and the sun has come out to play!"

Who would you rather sit next to in a café?

UNIT 34: ASSERTIVENESS

This does not mean being AGGRESSIVE in the workplace.

It means that even if you are shy, you will be able to stand up for yourself and volunteer for new and additional work roles with enthusiasm.

Do you consider yourself to be assertive? What does being assertive mean to you?

Does it mean exercising your rights all the time, every time? Or does it mean knowing when to let someone else or some other cause or outcome take precedence over your rights?

For example: is the boss who places a pile of work on an employee's desk the afternoon before that employee goes on vacation, being assertive? Or, is the employee who is about to go on vacation being assertive when she tells the boss that the work will be done upon his/her return?

It's not always easy to identify truly assertive behaviour. This is because there is a fine line between assertiveness and aggression. So some definitions are helpful when trying to separate the two:

Assertiveness is based on balance - it requires being forthright about your wants and needs while still considering the rights, needs, and wants of others. When you are assertive, you ask for what you want but you don't necessarily get it.

Aggressive behaviour is based on winning - it requires that you do what is in your own best interest without regard for the rights, needs, feelings or desires of others. When you are aggressive, you take what you want regardless, and you don't usually ask.

So, that boss was being aggressive. Yes, he had work that needed to be done. However, by dumping it on his employee at such an inappropriate time, he showed a total lack of regard for the needs and feelings of his employee.

The employee, on the other hand, demonstrated assertive behaviour by informing the boss that the work **would** be done, but it would be done on return from vacation. The employee's rights were asserted while recognizing the boss's need to get the job done.

Assertiveness is not necessarily easy, but it is a skill that can be learned. Developing your assertiveness starts with a good understanding of who you are and a belief in the value you bring. When you have that, you have the basis of <u>self-confidence</u>. Assertiveness helps to build on that self-confidence and provides many other benefits for improving your relationships at work and in other areas of your life as well. In general, assertive people:

- Get to 'win-win' more easily – they see the value in their opponent and in his/her position, and can quickly find common ground;

- Are better problem solvers – they feel empowered to do whatever it takes to find the best solution;

- Are less stressed – they know they have personal power and they don't feel threatened or victimised when things don't go as planned or expected;

- Are doers – they get things done because they know they can.

When you act assertively you act fairly and with empathy. The power you use comes from your self-assurance and not from intimidation or bullying. When you treat others with such fairness and respect, you get that same treatment in return. You are well liked and people see you as a leader and someone they want to work with.

Developing Your Assertiveness

Some people are naturally more assertive than others. If your disposition tends more towards being either passive or aggressive, you need to work on the following skills to develop your assertiveness.

Value yourself and your rights:

- Understand that your rights, thoughts, feelings, needs and desires are just as important as everyone else's;

- But remember they are not more important than anyone else's, either;

- Recognise your rights and protect them;

- Believe you deserve to be treated with respect and dignity at all times;

- Stop apologizing for everything.

Identify your needs and wants, and ask for them to be satisfied:

- Don't wait for someone to recognise what you need (you might wait forever!);

- Understand that to perform to your full potential, your needs must be met;

- Find ways to get your needs met without sacrificing others' needs in the process.

Acknowledge that people are responsible for their own behaviour:

- Don't make the mistake of accepting responsibility for how people react to your assertive statements (e.g. anger, resentment). You can only control yourself;

- As long as you are not violating someone else's needs, then you have the right to say or do what you want.

Express negative thoughts and feelings in a healthy and positive manner:

- Allow yourself to be angry, but always be respectful;
- Do say what's on your mind, but do it in a way that protects the other person's feelings;
- Control your emotions;
- Stand up for yourself and confront people who challenge you and/or your rights.

Receive criticism and compliments positively:

- Accept compliments graciously;
- Allow yourself to make mistakes and ask for help;
- Accept feedback positively – be prepared to say you don't agree but do not get defensive or angry.

Learn to say "No" when you need to. This is the granddaddy of assertiveness!

- Know your limits and what will cause you to feel taken advantage of;

- Know that you can't do everything or please everyone and learn to be OK with that;
- Go with what is right for you;
- Suggest an alternative for a win-win solution.

Assertive Communication Techniques

There are a variety of ways to communicate assertively. By understanding how to be assertive, you can quickly adapt these techniques to any situation you are facing.

I: Statements

Use "I want ...", "I need ..." or "I feel ..." to convey basic assertions:

I feel strongly that we need to bring in a third party to mediate this disagreement.

Empathic Assertion

First, recognise how the other person views the situation:

I understand you are having trouble working with Arlene.

Then, express what you need:

...however, this project needs to be completed by Friday. Let's all sit down and come up with a plan to get it done.

Escalating Assertion

This type of assertiveness is necessary when your first attempts are not successful in getting your needs met.

The technique involves getting more and more firm as time goes on. It may end in you telling the person what you will do next if you do not receive satisfaction. Remember, though, regardless of the consequences you give, you may not get what you want in the end.

John, this is the third time this week I've had to speak to you about arriving late. If you are late one more time this month, I will activate the disciplinary process.

Ask For More Time

Sometimes, you just need to put off saying anything. You might be too emotional or you might really not know what you want. Be honest and tell the person you need a few minutes to compose your thoughts.

Dave, your request has caught me off guard. I'll get back to you within the half hour.

Change Your Verbs

- Use 'won't' instead of 'can't';
- Use 'want' instead of 'need';
- Use 'choose to' instead of 'have to';
- Use 'could' instead of 'should'.

Broken Record

Prepare ahead of time the message you want to convey:

I cannot take on any more projects right now.

During the conversation, keep restating your message using the same language over and over again. Don't relent. Eventually the person is likely to realise that you really mean what you are saying.

- I would like you to work on the Clancy project.

    I cannot take on any more projects right now.

- I'll pay extra for you accommodating me.

    I cannot take on any more projects right now.

- Seriously, this is really important; my boss insists this gets done.

    I cannot take on any more projects right now.

- Will you do it as a personal favour?

    I'm sorry, I value our past relationship but I simply cannot take on any more projects right now.

Tip:

Be careful with the broken record technique. If you use it to protect yourself from exploitation, that's good. However, if you use it to bully someone into taking action that's against their interests, it's manipulative, dishonest and bad.

Scripting

This technique involves preparing your responses using a four-pronged approach that describes:

1. **The event:** tell the other person exactly how you see the situation or problem.

    Jacob, the production costs this month are 23% higher than average. You didn't give me any indication of this, which meant that I was completely surprised by the news.

2. **Your feelings:** describe how you feel about expressing your emotions clearly.

    This frustrates me and makes me feel like you don't understand or appreciate how important financial controls are in the company.

3. **Your needs:** tell the other person what you need so they don't have to guess.

    I need you to be honest with me and let me know when we start going significantly over budget on anything.

4. **The consequences:** describe the positive outcome if your needs are fulfilled.

    I'm here to help you and support you in any way I can. If you trust me, then together we can turn this around.

Once you are clear about what you want to say and express, it is much easier to actually do it.

Key Points

Being assertive means knowing where the fine line is between assertion and aggression and balancing on it. It means having a strong sense of yourself and acknowledging that you deserve to get what you want. It means standing up for yourself even in the most difficult situations.

Assertiveness can be learned and developed, and although it won't happen overnight, by practising the techniques presented here you will slowly become more confident in expressing your needs and wants. As your assertiveness improves, so will your productivity and efficiency. Start today and begin to see how being assertive allows you to work with people to accomplish tasks, solve problems, and reach solutions.

One of the biggest problems we have in communicating is feeling comfortable by saying 'NO'- particularly for women. Try it and mean it - Assert your new Assertiveness!

UNIT 35: ACTION PLANS

Every Sunday afternoon I create a weekly ACTION PLAN that I work from to achieve what I need to do to complete that working week. Most Motivational Speakers do the same, from Tony Robbins to Richard Templar - The Rules of Work.

I list them from 1-20 in order of importance and prioritise what I need to achieve that week. I put an asterisk (*) against those which require IMMEDIATE ATTENTION and I work through them accordingly.

I also have Short Term, Medium Term and Long Term Goals set into this as I work my way through the weeks.

Each January I set myself 10 achievable GOALS and in 2012 I achieved 8 out of 10 which I was proud of, considering I did not work for a considerable time as I had a parent that was ill.

Try not to be too hard on yourself (as I am on myself), but be realistic.

WEEKLY ACTIONPLAN/BUSINESS STRATEGY FOR 2013

Example One

DATE	OBJECTIVES - AIM	ACTION - HOW	PRIORITY 1 to 4	MILESTONES	OUTCOMES
JAN 2013– Week 1 **Wed2 Jan**	Work on Mentor's ACTION PLAN	Advice – mentors/ research	1	Consultancy work	Move nearer to achieving my goals, ready for May meeting
Thurs 3 Jan					
Fri 4 Jan					
Sat 5 Jan					
Sun 6 Jan					
Mon 7 Jan					
Tues 8 Jan					

Example Two

NOTE PAD

ACTION PLANFOR W/C23 APRIL 2012

1. Look for suitable premises – TICK this off when complete and give it a * if it is a PRIORITY for the week

2.

3.

4.

5.

6.

7.

8.

9.

10.

Refer to this every day and work from this. On the Friday, make sure you have achieved all those marked with a *. Do not move forward to the following week UNLESSTHESE HAVE BEEN ACHIEVED – you would then be in deep trouble for not nailing your tasks.

Action Plan Daily

(Listed in order of priority – remember **time management**)

You should start your working week with a 7 am rise with breathing exercises, then a 10 minute exercise plan followed by light healthy breakfast. Wash and dress and be ready for a working day. Sample of my day;

1. Clear out emails and respond;

2. Send 5 speculative emails to success stories that I have read about over the weekend;

3. Application 1 – Social Network Board.

Each day you should break for a light lunch and a good walk.

1. Visit to solicitors, dentist, doctors;

2. Try to create contacts – email or phone;

3. 2nd application;

4. Re-evaluate CV, letters and personal profile;

5. After 10am visit all **job sites** eg.Councils etc. and note job vacancies;

6. Social Networking Event – Liverpool – Fundraising Event – BT;

7. Gym – banking;

8. **Job club** – family/home/leisure activity;

9. Support family members and prepare **Action Plan** for following week.

Additional Tips

Look up old work colleagues, check local council sites and agencies for successful tenders to demonstrate NEW contracts.

TIME MANAGEMENT

HOW?

1. **Time Is Money**: You can make money- you can't make time. An inch of gold cannot buy an inch of time.

2. **Why Time Management**? To utilise the available time in an optimum manner to achieve one's personal and professional goals.

3. **Time for Everything**:

   - Take time to work, it is the price of success;

   - Take time to think; it is the source of power;

   - Take time to play; it is the source of youth;

   - Take time to read; it is the source of wisdom;

   - Take time to love; it is the privilege of God;

   - Take time to serve; it is the purpose of life;

   - Take time to laugh; it is the music of soul and sometimes we forget to smile - laugh and have fun!

4. **How to Live on 24 Hours a Day**: The title of Arnold Bennett's book, published in 1907. Henry Ford gave 500 copies of the book to his managers; the president of another American motor company issued 18,000 copies – one to each employee.

5. **Time Awareness – Time Tracking**: Peter Drucker "Make sure you know where your time goes". Don't depend on memory. Keep a time log. See that your time is spent as per your priorities or your core responsibilities.

6. **Managers' Time**: Planning is the key managerial function, but research shows that less than 5% of management time goes on planning. Pareto Principle: 20% of your time will produce 80% of your productive output; can you afford not to manage at least that 20% ?Parkinson's Law: work expands to fill the time available for it. Beware!

7. **Time Management Matrix**: Classify activities by Urgency / Importance:

   egg   URGENT / NOT URGENT   (1-2)

            NOT IMPORTANT   (3-4).

8. **Efficiency versus Effectiveness**: Often the worst performers are those who seem to be working hardest and longest; they may be very busy but not necessarily effective.

9. **Common time Management Problems-Procrastination**: Putting off the doing of something intentionally and habitually. If you suspect yourself, ask yourself – why am I putting this off? If there is no reason, do it. Do not confuse reason with excuse - procrastination is the world's number one time waster. Banish it from your life

as there is no time like the present to do any work.

10. **Common Time Management Problems - Poor Delegation**: Delegation implies transferring initiative and authority to another - do not spend time on work that can be done, to a satisfactory level, by someone else. Delegation saves your time and develops subordinates, and can improve results by making fuller use of resources.

11. **The Art of Delegation**: Delegation begins with a deep sense of the value and limits of your time. Managers often complain that they are running out of time when their subordinates are running out of work. Delegating the more routine or predictable part of one's job is only the first step - delegation is not abdication, but some degree of control needs to be maintained.

12. **Difficulties in Delegation**: It can be risky. We enjoy doing things. We don't sit and think. It's a slow process. We like to be 'on top of everything'. Will our subordinate outstrip us? Nobody can do it as well as I can. However, delegation is a great motivator which enriches jobs, improves performance and raises staff morale.

13. **Common Time Management Problems - Office Mismanagement**: Develop an efficient system of office working. Muddle makes work and wastes time, so strive for good order in your office. Utilise all resources fully. Handle the telephone properly; don't let it become a nuisance. As

often as possible, handle a piece of paper only once.

14. **Time Effectiveness in Offices:** Time can be wasted imperceptibly if your work area is not organised well. Your desk should be clear of all paper except the specific job on hand. It invites you to think about one thing at a time. Concentration is a great time saver. Paperwork: the recommended principle is 'to handle each piece of paper only once'. Sort papers under:

- FOR ACTION
- FOR INFORMATION
- FOR READING
- FOR WASTE PAPER
- FOR BOTTOM DRAWER.

15. **Effective Emails**: Clarity, simplicity and conciseness are essentials of good writing. Think, List and then Arrange. Do not cover too many subjects in one letter. Strive to write one page letter, which are more digestible.

16. **Make the Telephone Work for You**: The telephone is a great time-saving tool in the right hands. So plan your calls by setting aside a period of time for making and if possible, receiving calls, timing each call. Emails are the worst curse ever and not kind to time management.

17. **How to Control Interruptions:** Set a time limit and stick to it. Set the stage in advance: e.g. you are very busy with a deadline in sight, so with casual droppers-in, remain standing and get visitors quickly to the point. Meet in the other person's office. Be ruthless with time but gracious with people. Have a clock available, and use a call-back system for telephone calls.

18. You are your own **Virtual PA**.

19. **Common Time Management Problems - Meetings**: Meetings are a necessary evil but are potential time wasters and can be distractions from one's regular work. Try to say 'No' to a meeting where you are not required. Make sure there is a definite Agenda, which everyone should receive along with relevant papers well in advance. Ensure there is a set finishing time for each meeting.

20. **Dos and Don'ts for Boss / Chairperson / Administrator**: Do not call a meeting unless it is necessary, or if the task can be handled by a call or by a small group through formal/informal discussion. Meetings are not required to: 'Mess you around or confuse you.

21. **More Dos and Don'ts for Boss / Chairperson / Administrator**: Call only those who are involved, and have a written agenda and circulate to all along with supporting papers. Do not over-pack the agenda and exclude 'Any other item'.

Start on time and stick to the agenda. Beware of 'hijackers'.

22. **Dos and Don'ts for Participants**: Come prepared with facts and figures and arrive on time. Talk to the point and do not try to divert the discussion or hijack the meeting.

23. **Boss-Imposed Time**: Time spent doing things we would not be doing if we did not have bosses. Keeping bosses satisfied takes time, but dealing with dissatisfied bosses takes even more time. Failing to invest sufficient time to satisfy bosses always results in more and more boss-imposed time, with less time for others.

24. **Role of Boss**: Boss must realise that the time of the subordinate is also important for the organisation. The tasks monitored by you are only part of the duties of the subordinate. If the subordinate is hard pressed for time, the quality of the output is bound to suffer. System improvements are essential responsibilities of bosses-particularly those which reduce time being spent on unimportant/unnecessary activities. You can do only one person's work. Perfection, at times, becomes counterproductive.

25. **Planning the Day**: Prepare a list of priorities for the day based on urgency and importance. Get the timing right. Morning is the time for hard work. Interesting work, meetings and social events can take place in off-peak time. Have work-breaks

to overcome fatigue. Living 100% in the present improves your work output.

26. **Other Time Savers**:

- Concentration;
- Avoid interruptions;
- Use of committed time;
- Good health;
- Do not let your subordinate come to you with problems unless they bring their proposed solutions.

27. **Problems of the Overworked Manager**: Why some managers are typically running out of time while their staff is running out of work:

- they pick up their staffs' jobs;
- they enjoy and are good at it;
- they try to do things efficiently which are not worth doing in the first place.

Efficiency vs Effectiveness can be explained by the 'Monkey-on-the-back' analogy. The Monkey is the 'next move' or problem or opportunity that comes to us.

28. **What is a Monkey?:** A monkey is a next move, an opportunity, or a problem which comes to us. 'Monkey Management' helps to transform a manager under time pressure into an effective one.

29. **Monkey-on-the-Back**: Sometimes colleagues try to pass on their monkeys eg. many bosses are in the habit of passing their monkeys on to subordinates. This snowballs upwards, sideways and downwards –becoming 'Leaping Monkeys'. These take our all available time with no time to work on our own 'Monkeys', so be careful not to accept others' monkeys.

30. **Recap 1:**

   - Yesterday is a cancelled cheque; tomorrow is a promissory note; today is ready cash - use it.

   - When feasible, delegate.

   - Don't let paperwork pile up.

   - Do not postpone work.

   - Identify your time wasters and resolve to eliminate them.

   - Add times for relaxation and recreation into your schedule.

31. **Recap 2**

   - Identify and make use of 'up' and 'down' time

   - Learn to say "NO" - it is not a crime.

   - Make use of committed time – travel time, waiting time etc.

   - Plan the day.

- Set goals and work towards achieving them.
- Keep the Boss happy.

<u>YOU</u> manage Time – Time does not manage <u>YOU</u>!

UNIT 36: EMPLOYMENT STRATEGY

This will reflect your Short, Middle and Long Term Goals for the year.

Please review these every Quarter to keep on track.

EMPLOYMENT STRATEGY UNTIL 2013

DATE	OBJECTIVES – AIM	ACTION - HOW	PRIORITIES 1 to 4	MILESTONES	OUTCOMES
Nov 4 13	CV x 2 – Personal Profile	Advice – mentors and job club	1	IT Access	Polished CV etc
Nov 4 13	Have coffee with Mentor				
Nov 4 13	Voluntary Placement				
Nov 4 13	ACTION PLAN/ STRATEGY				
Nov 11 13	Practice with partner Interview Techniques				
Nov 11 13	Increase Spec Emails x10				
Nov 18 13	Review – Interview Technique and learn from the DVD				

Nov 18 13	Increase Social Networking x 2 events				
Nov 25 13	Update knowledge of keeping a job				
Nov 25 13	Join another Networking Club and Agency				

UNIT 37: PERSONAL CAREER DEVELOPMENT PLAN

For Professionals and Executives this comes now, after your contact details at the beginning of your CV. You would set this up once you have nailed your job and plan your future around it - as we all want promotion and need this type of strategy to demonstrate evidence base when attending Appraisals.

PERSONAL CAREER DEVELOPMENT PLAN – ROCK STAR YOUTH 2013

OBJECTIVE/ TARGET/ BASED ON JD/SPEC	ACTION/TASKS TO DELIVER	WHO	BY WHEN	SOURCES OF HELP
Jan 2013 - Secure Events across NW/NE UK	Use my contacts to contact and visit and set these up with our partners	ALL NW Business 18-30 Contacts Universities	April 2013	Other Partners Colleges Enterprise Trusts etc.

UNIT 38: LEADERSHIP AND MANAGEMENT

These notes are based on the NHS Leadership Framework Model.
state what the following mean:

- self belief
- self awareness
- self management
- drive for improvement
- personal integrity.

An extract from the NWDA – Northwest Regional Economic Strategy 2006:

To develop leadership, management and enterprise skills and develop world class management/ leadership and corporate social responsibility/ environmental management skills by:

- focussing support on managers of companies looking to grow and first line management/supervisory staff with no formal management training.

-   developing the Northern Leadership Academy, strengthening the network of Leadership Centres and Development Programmes, and developing mentoring opportunities.

Research

This indicates that management/leadership and work organisation skills are crucial for companies, ensuring the skills/ideas of the whole workforce are used effectively. Key issues include developing the demand for leadership skills and considering making leadership development a condition of taking up business support grants.

Suggested books to read

- Edward de Bono and Robert Heller, *Management Intelligence* – sign up for email alerts.

- Richard Branson and Warren Buffett, *Thinking Manager Style* – this is the one I personally would go for!

- Richard Branson, *British Entrepreneur*. The Virgin Group has over 200 companies in entertainment, media and travel; with an estimated fortune of £4 billion he certainly made the Rich List 2006.

Having worked and professionally interacted with NHS.NWDA and Richard Branson I will most definitely go for Richard Branson as it is hands on.

Get things done now, not later, and delegate!

Richard Branson puts his success down to **time management skills** and feels that, in the beginning, the following skills are crucial to leadership qualities:

- upbringing – stand on your own two feet;
- character building – endurance;
- believe 100% in yourself;
- be proud;
- strong personality;
- build from scratch;
- trial and error;
- time management skills – 1/3 on trouble shooting,1/3 on new projects (charitable/business) and 1/3 on marketing;
- time for family – holiday and friends;
- social responsibility;
- delegation;
- caring personality – people matter - if you like people, it will bring out the best in them;
- step back;
- the department/company must be able to operate smoothly without you!

Management Skills

We will focus on two types of Management Styles and you decide what you are more comfortable with – if any at all!

Predictive management skills

To prevent problems and focus on problems not arising

You tend to be:

- thoughtful
- analytical
- not looking for dramas/problems
- able to concentrate on what is happening at present
- what is important
- can identify patterns of errors
- more focussed on what went wrong
- have a need to fix it
- always look at the bigger picture
- work through all the details.

If you have the above qualities then you are a DETACHED person who can identify and implement, relate and link to the early warning signs.

Reactive management skills

Solves problems as they occur and gets resources back on track

You tend to be:

- decisive
- act quickly
- find solutions
- creative
- create solutions
- innovative
- calm
- in control
- analytical.

You can be both the above, or you could start off as a reactive manage and develop into a predictive manager.

Exercise- are you a good manager?

Need to get better at predictive management? So practise!

You had a problem at work: what happened? Any signs? What did you do? What could you have done to prevent it? What can you do to prevent it happening again?

A good manager continually monitors to flag up warning signs and then evaluates results. Learn from your skills as a reactive manager - put your resources into 'getting things done'. In preventive management – give yourself time to think.

So, what type of Manager are you?

ILM Level 7 Diploma - Executive Management and Strategic Leadership

I am a Fellow of ILM and deliver to Level 7 which is an Executive Level.

Who is this qualification for? This is a challenging programme, designed to develop leadership skills at the most senior level. It is best suited to practising senior managers with significant experience. Learners will be able to benchmark their skills, accredit their experience and develop themselves professionally.

Benefits for individuals:

- Get a thorough grounding in the role of senior management;

- Understand the influence of different theories and models on management practice;

- Make strong, informed decisions using a range of strategies;

- Analyse the principles and practice of leadership in their organisation;

- Critically evaluate their own performance as a leader;

- Acquire the tools, skills and knowledge to take responsibility for their professional development.

Benefits for employers:

- Prepare and groom future leaders for the organisation;

- Benchmark the skills and knowledge of their most senior managers;

- Produce senior managers who understand strategic leadership in the context of their organisation;

- Produce senior managers who are self-aware and take responsibility for self-development;

- The range of optional units means this qualification can be tailored to individual needs: close skills gaps, develop and shape a talent pipeline in the organisation.

This qualification includes units that focus on the practical skills individuals need at this level; units that will build specialist business knowledge and units that are designed to help learners take responsibility for their own development.

There are six mandatory units:

- 'Developing the Executive Manager'
- 'Making Informed Decisions'
- 'Leadership in Practice'
- 'Developing the Reflective Leader'
- 'The Leadership Journey'
- 'Leading Change in Organisations'.

There is also a wide range of optional units, so the qualification can be tailored to the learner's individual requirements.

Progression: Successful completion of these qualifications can lead to a range of progression options at a suitable level within or outside the Qualifications and Credit Framework.

Tasks

Based on the above - I am going to work with you in two groups to cover the six mandatory Units above.

I am going to ask you to appoint your Leader or someone to put themselves up for the Leader. Then on TASK 2 I will ask you if they led well and if you wish to change your Leader or see whether someone else wants to try leading the challenge.

I will give you two real life Organisational Situations that have happened to me in my Career:

Task One

A member of your Team. who has been with you for 15 years and was a valid TEAM MEMBER, has recently had a bereavement and thus has over the last year had a considerable amount of time off and arrives late and is letting the team down. There have been reports of drinking alcohol at work and bottles of spirits have been found in the filing room and in other places. The burden of the workload on the team is not durable and your Head of Department has asked you to deal with the situation satisfactorily for all.

Task Two

You run events across the NW and upon checking the venues have noted that your Department has been paying for venues that have remained empty for the past year. Therefore, your team have not been populating the venues and thus you have been losing revenue - paying for empty venues and paying for contracts - yearly up front and losing revenue from not running programmes for which you are paying £400 per person. Find a solution that will have an improvement on your Departmental budget.

Presentations

Each Leader presents the *Solution* to the above Tasks and the other team members make comments; then both Teams will decide who led more *Strategically* and the *Management Style* and then discuss who would be promoted as Leaders / Managers and who are *Good Team Players*.

Did you find out what type of MANAGER you are?

Are you a natural LEADER?

Are you a TEAM PLAYER?

Can a LEADER be an effective MANAGER?

Are you both a LEADER and a MANAGER?

Where you born a LEADER?

Can you become a LEADER and MANAGER?

If you can demonstrate that you can deliver all of the above then you are an EXECUTIVE MANAGER and STRATEGIC LEADER - you are now ready to take on that new role!

UNIT 39: INTRODUCTION TO INTERVIEW TECHNIQUES

Interview Techniques - Steps 1 to 24 :'Get the job you deserve'!

You are advised to have a **strategy** for this and can use various methods:

- **Behavioural**
- **NLP (Neuro-Linguistic Programming)**
- **Emotional intelligence.**

Or why not combine all of the above:

I am going to take you through this **last but one hurdle in steps**. Personally, I feel this is the most nerve-racking and unpredictable experience of the whole procedure of securing a job.

Step 1

You receive confirmation of your interview in writing by post, letter, email, telephone call, text or in person.

Action: Confirmation

If you ring to confirm, please speak to the person directly and follow this up in writing by letter or email **thanking** them for inviting you and **confirming** the correct date, day, time and place. **Ask** for directions and best possible means of transport ie.parking etc. so you can plan your journey. **Ask** who is on the panel, their names, titles etc. to research these people within or outside the organisation. **Ask** about the format of the **interview, presentation title** – clarify this with them and check on how much time has been allocated to this as part of the interview. **Ask** how long the interview will be. **Ask** how many candidates they are interviewing and if there will be second or even third interviews. **Ask** if anyone is being interviewed who is internal or on redeployment. **Ask** if they want to see any additional information i.e. certificates.

Step 2 -Action: Research the company

Go to the company website, research the people who are interviewing you and even call them for additional information or just to familiarise yourself with their voice, note their response to questions and information given. Do you know anyone in the organisation who can give you some internal politics on the Team, Department and Company etc?

Know as much as possible about the people and the company before you go:

- products/services
- new areas of investment

- their vision
- development
- structure
- you now have LinkedIn to search for the people who are involved in that Company within their Group to do this research.

Do you fit in? **Ask** someone who already works there.

What is **corporate integrity?** Visit one morning and watch who goes in, the style of clothes, type of person and SPOT any trend or branding going on. If you are not local, then use LinkedIn to follow them through their Groups and, of course, their updates re: their website - via their blogging and tweets.

You want to fit in!

Step 3 -Action: Think Positively

This is the physiological approach to the interview. Think positively about the organisation, the people and your JOBROLE.

Step 4 -Action: Create an Impression

This is all about impression. Remember that the first impression is the lasting impression! Again, from doing your research or visiting the company you will see what the **corporate dress code** is and what is not appropriate.

Clothes

Go to your **corporate wardrobe** and coordinate the outfit to suit the image, being comfortable to suit the weather. A good colour choice is black, navy blue or grey teamed with white, red or purple to make an impact. Does your suit need to go to the dry cleaners? Do it now! Should you buy a new shirt/top to make you feel good about yourself, because you are worth it? Shoes – are they in good condition, do they need to be heeled? Accessories – do not over do it; that goes for jewellery, scarves etc. too. Files – do you have a briefcase or a case trolley? Do not use a plastic shopping bag, please.

Step 5 -Action: Preparation

Make sure you prepare for the journey, do a dummy run and time it – it is better to be early than too late. If it is not possible to run through this, calculate the journey on www.google.com; if it takes three hours to get there by rail - then double it - always be prepared and phone them in advance if there are any delays.

Step 6 -Action: Swot Up

The night before the interview, read through the **Job Description, Job Specification** and other information you have collected. Concentrate on the Job Specification because it is using a point system as in NHS search and selection. So for each point on the Job Specification you will be asked a question and your answer will be expected to mirror what you put in your Application Form. Give them a solid demonstration of evidence for that in relation to your last position, always thinking what skills/ qualities you will be bringing to their organisation. If you are preparing a **presentation** using **PowerPoint,** check that their facilities are compatible with your IT package to make sure you save it in the right format. If you have not done PowerPoint for a while, go onto an online course or ask a friend to take you through it – there's nothing worse than at the start of the interview coming across as 'tacky' and unprofessional.

Step 7 -Action: Relaxation

The night before, have a relaxing bath, go to bed early and think positively. Before going to sleep tell yourself **'this job is mine'.** Take some deep breaths and off you go!

- Wake up extra early, have a power shower – a shot of cold water will get your reactive skills going;

- Have a light breakfast and relax;

- Have a check list of what should be in your briefcase's, Job Description, Job Specification, your certificates and proof of ID;details of where you are going and how to get there; name of organisation, address and contact telephone numbers. Take a pen and pad for notes, and a laptop if needed. Take your mobile phone but do not forget to switch it off or put it on to silent mode before the interview;

- Leave in plenty time – remember you have done this journey so you have left yourself plenty of time. If it takes one hour to get there – then give yourself two.

I always send my presentation over prior to the interview; the day before I print off a copy and put a copy on my pen drive and take my laptop – technology has been known to let you down so many times.

If it is raining, take that umbrella – there's nothing worse than arriving looking as though you have been 'shipwrecked'!

Step 8 -Action: On Arrival

Arrive 15 minutes before the interview, introduce yourself and ask for the person concerned. You are now ONA STAGE so be nice to everyone, smile and think about what you say and do. You can read company literature while you wait, go to the bathroom, freshen up and take some deep breaths – whatever relaxes you.

Step 9 -Action: Body Language

Sit up straight, stand up straight and smile! Don't smile and shake everyone's hand (including the cleaner's), though!

Step 10 -Action: First Impression

Give a firm handshake, making sure your palms are dry, give a warm smile, but keep it relaxed. Sit comfortably, get yourself organised, have a glass of water if offered one and you are ready to SELL YOURSELF!

Step 11 -Action: Sell Yourself

You are now on stage/on show and you have two minutes to make your lasting impression. Go on –you OWN it!

Remember the names and positions of your interviewers and always give direct eye contact to the person who asks the questions.

Step 12 -Action: Timing

Most interviews run from 20 minutes to 1 hour so watch the pace of the interview, which will be set by the interviewers. Be aware of the answers you give and do not repeat or waffle.

Step 13 -Action: Influence

You must influence from start to finish and stay in control.

Step 14 -Action: Rapport

Engage and create a rapport with the interviewer/s (there can be between one to twelve people on a panel; however three is average, usually head of the department, a HR representative and the person who you would report to).

Step 15 -Action: Pacing

Do not rush or drag out the interview and let them decide when to finish. Even your voice should be paced throughout the interview.

Step 16 -COMPETENCY BASED Q/A

Action: Questions/answers

Here are some common ones that keep coming up:

Q   What attracted you to this job?

Q   What qualities can you bring to this job?

Q   Give a brief summary of your career to date

Q   What do you think we do as an organisation and what is our vision?

Q   How do you ensure that monthly reports are completed on time?

Q   How do you ensure that the team members email to you the information you need for the monthly report deadlines?

Your answers will attract a score (sample):SEARCH AND SELECTION

1 excellent
2 good
3 basic

4 poor
0 not applicable

Step 17 -Action: Answers

For all of your answers, be prepared to give an example and evidence to back your response and relate it to your last job if possible.

Step 18 -Action: Listen

Always listen and influence all of the interviewers but weigh up who carries the casting vote!

Step 19 -Action: Do you fit in?

Even though you are thinking positively throughout the interview, form a judgement of your own – do you fit in and do you want to fit in? To do this, value their eye contact and body language.

Step 20 -Action: Interpret the interviewers' needs

Read the signals - give them what they want to hear and not what you want to say.

Step 21 -Action: Influence

There are psychological influences taking part here and it is a technique which comes with practice and it helps to build rapport.

Step 22 -Action: Any Questions?

You should have some **Power Questions** prepared ready to ask - be aware of the time though.

Examples:

- Prospects for your own **personal development** within the organisation?

- **Career Progression** within the role and within the Team?

- Contract – how long and what kind of opportunities are there within the company?

I never ask more than three.

If you are brave and confident, which you should be by now - I always add in this question:

"If there is any doubt in your mind as to why I am not the best candidate for this position, please ask me your question now, so that I can assure you that I am!"

Step 23 -Action: Closure

Let the interviewers bring the interview to a close by stating when and how they will let you know.

Step 24 -Action: Thank You

Shake hands firmly and thank them for inviting you. Say it with a smile!

You should come out feeling on a high and positive that you have done your best and the outcome will be – YOU HAVE THAT JOB!

NOTES

Write your questions down and take notes if you have to (ask permission).

If you do not know the answer to a question, ask them to repeat it. If you are still unsure, ask them if you can return to that question at a later stage.

UNIT 40: WHAT HUMAN RESOURCES MANAGERS LOOK FOR

- Ability to do the job;
- Ability to make a contribution to effectiveness of organisation;
- Potential development.

Well done - you have worked hard on your CV/ application form and this has now paid off by getting you that important interview. Now you need to take the next step by getting suited and booted, plaster on that big smile and be ready to answer a number of questions so that you achieve that job.

HR have shortlisted all the candidates and the interview is an opportunity to assess each applicant. It is also an opportunity for the candidate to ask for more details about the job, the organisation and to make sure it is the right job for you.

Questions should mainly be focused around what you have written in your CV, so:

Be Honest

If you lie or embellish your CV, nine times out of ten you will be found out as there are tell-tale signs such as body language. If you are successful and land the job, your lie or embellishment will soon be found out once you are in the role and you could be dismissed.

Know Your CV

Be ready to answer questions on whatever you have written. The format of interviewing is normally based around open questions that start with:

WHO/WHAT/WHERE/WHEN/HOW?

Be Confident

Not all interviews are taken or attended by someone from HR. You may also be asked questions that you do not feel entirely comfortable with. If this happens and it makes you feel nervous or uncomfortable, take a deep breath before answering and decide how you want to answer. If necessary, ask them to repeat the question, or repeat it back to the person; you may have misheard what they said.

Chartered Institute of Personnel and Development Survey

In a survey conducted in May/June 2009 a number of HR members were asked what they looked for when filling a role. They said:

- Flexibility
- Fit with culture and values of the organisation.

UNIT 41: QUESTIONS - WHAT TO EXPECT

Opening Questions

- Tell me about yourself
- What do you enjoy most in your current job?
- Why have you applied for this position?
- Why do you want to leave your current job?
- What do you know about our company?
- What do you think is the role of a ....?
- What can you bring to this job?

Behavioural Questions

Tell me about a time you have....

- Worked as part of a team
- Handled conflict in a team
- Managed conflicting deadlines
- Dealt with a difficult customer

- Provided excellent customer service
- Managed a project through to completion
- Worked on your own initiative
- Disagreed with a colleague/your manager
- Managed a de-motivated member of staff
- Handled a performance issue in the workplace
- Worked under stress/pressure
- Had to handle criticism.

Follow up Questions

- Why did you deal with it in that way?
- What was the outcome?
- What would you do differently next time?
- What did you learn from that experience?
- What did you find most difficult about that situation?

Awkward Questions

- What are your strengths/weaknesses?
- How would your colleagues/boss/ friends describe you?

- What is your management style?

- What do you dislike about your current role?

- Why have you been with your current employer for such a long/short time?

- What are the key trends/developments in this industry?

- What is your current manager's greatest weakness?

- What salary are you expecting?

- What sort of decisions do you find most difficult?

More questions and the answers:

1. **Let's look at your CV**
   Have your CV handy to appraise your Career History for the last 10 years only.

2. **Tell me about yourself**
   Cover four segments about your life – your early years, education, work experience and what has been happening recently. Keep your complete answer to not more than two or three minutes. Be sure you do not ramble or elaborate.

3. **What can you offer us?**
   Be sure you know something about the job situation they have in mind before

you try to answer; then you can relate some of your past experiences, and where you have succeeded in solving problems that appear similar to those of your prospective employer.

4. **What are your strengths?**

By now you should be able to list and concisely explain three or four strengths that are relevant to their needs.

5. **What have you accomplished?**

Try to pick out accomplishments that relate to the challenges you have been discussing. Stay away from ancient times.

6. **What are your limitations?**

Respond with a strength which, if over-done, can get in your way and become a weakness. For example, you might say, "My ambition to get the job done sometimes causes me to press a little hard on my organisation. But I am aware of this problem and believe that I have it under control". Or deal with your need for further training in some aspect of your profession. Do not claim to be faultless.

7. **How much are you worth?**

Try to delay answering this until you have learned quite a bit about the job and, if possible, explore beforehand the typical salary ranges they are accustomed to pay for similar positions.

If you feel obliged to answer something, you might reply along these lines:"You are aware of what I have been earning at 'Ajax', and I would hope that coming with you would be a progressive step. Perhaps we can discuss this question a little better when we both have a more complete idea of what the job responsibilities and scope would be".

8. **What are your ambitions for the future?**

   Indicate your desire to concentrate on doing the immediate job well and that you are confident the future will take care of itself. You do not want to convey the idea that you have no desire to progress, but you need to avoid statements that are unrealistic – or that might threaten some of the present incumbents.

9. **What do you know about our company?**

   If you have done your homework, you can honestly state that you have studied the information that is publicly available about the company and are thus aware of several of the published facts. However, you might also state that you would like to know more – and then be prepared later to ask some intelligent questions.

Do not try to show off and recite all you have learned, but merely let your knowledge show gracefully through the informed way in which you handle the interview.

10. Why do you want to work for us?

Indicate that from your study of the company, many of the activities and problems would give you a clear chance to contribute to the company through past experience and skills. If you can honestly say so, explain your admiration for the company and what it is that appeals to you.

11. What do you find most attractive about the position we are discussing? What is least attractive?

Mention three or more attractive factors, but hold the unattractive down to one or two minor ones.

12. What do you look for in this job?

Keep your answer opportunity orientated. Talk about the chance you would have to perform and get recognition.

13. Please give me your definition of a .... (the position for which you are being interviewed)

Keep you answer brief and task orientated – that is, deal with responsibilities and accountabilities.

14. How long would it take you to make a meaningful contribution to our firm?

Be realistic and speak in terms of six months to a year.

15. Do you not feel you might be over qualified or too experienced for the position we have in mind?

A strong company needs strong people, with the appropriate experience to deal with current problems. Explain that your interest in the company would be long term, and that you are willing to bet that your accomplishments in the first year or two will lead eventually to growth opportunities for you.

16. What is your management style?

If you have not thought about this, it is time you did. If the job you are going for has management responsibilities, you might want to talk about how you set goals and then get your people involved in them. Also, describe the techniques that you like to use to bring out the best in people. Try to sense whether the company believes in a highly participative style or a more military approach.

17. Why do you feel you have good potential as a manager?

Keep your answers orientated towards your past achievements and the task to be done. Explain how you go about getting work done – either by yourself or through your organisation.

18. As a manager, what would you be looking for when you recruit people?

Their skills, initiative, adaptability and whether their chemistry fits with that of the organisation.

19. As a manager, have you ever had to terminate anyone's contract? If so, what were the circumstances and how did you handle it?

Answer in brief that you have indeed had experience with this problem and that it has worked out to the benefit of both the individual and the organisation.

20. What do you see as the most difficult task in being a manager?

Getting things planned and done on time, within the budget.

21. What important trends do you see coming in our industry?

Pick out two or three things that you see coming in the future and comment on the bigger picture. This is your chance to show that you have thought about the future, the economics, the markets and the technology of the industry.

22. Why are you leaving your present job?

This is one of those sensitive questions that must be handled crisply and briefly. If it was a workforce reduction owing to economic circumstances, make that clear. If possible, explain how your termination was part of a larger movement. When you have finished answering, let it go. Stay away from analysing any areas of friction with your boss.

23. How do you feel about leaving all your benefits at ....?

Concerned, but confident that you will make it up when you are established in your new company.

24. Describe what you feel would be an ideal working environment?

This is a place where you can bring in some satisfiers and ideal job preferences – but do not make it sound too sublime or impractical. Otherwise, they may conclude that you are not ready for the realities. Play down the dissatisfies.

25. Looking back, how do you perceive your past employer?

It is an excellent company which has given me a lot of good experience and opportunities to perform.

26. What have you done that helped increase sales or profit? How did you go about it?

This is your chance to describe in some detail a business accomplishment that is relevant to the proposed new job. Feel free to dwell on this.

27. How much financial responsibility have you had to account for?

You can answer this in terms of your budget or head-count or the size of the project or sales that you directed.

28. How many people have you supervised in your recent jobs?

Be specific – and feel free to refer to those over which you had influence, such as a task force or matrix organisation.

29. Which do you like better –working with figures or words?

Answer honestly.

30. How do you think your subordinates perceive you?

Be as positive as you can, but remember to be honest too. They can check your references easily.

31. In your last position, what were the things that you liked most? And liked least?

Be careful here. Emphasise the positive and do not carry on at length about the negative.

32. In your recent position, what were some of your most significant accomplishments?

Be ready to describe three or four of them in detail. Where possible, try to relate to the nature of the new challenges you might be facing.

33. Why have you not found a new position after these many months?

Finding just any job is not too difficult, but finding the right job takes care and time.

34. What do you think of your previous boss?

Be as positive as you can, and avoid getting in too deeply. This is a loaded question, because most bosses shy

away from a contentious or difficult
subordinate.

35. Describe a situation in which your work was criticised?

Be specific and brief – avoid getting
emotional or defensive about it.

36. If I spoke with your previous boss, what would he say are your greatest strengths and weaknesses?

Be honest about this one, but do not
emphasise the negative. Your old boss
will probably want to give you a good
send off. Recount some of the good
things you did for him/her.

37. How do you hold up under pressure or deadlines?

I can handle it. It's a way of life in the
business world.

38. Do you think you are cut out better for staff work or line work?

I can handle either, and my preference
depends a lot on the specific job, the
boss I would be working for, and the
challenges in the position.

39. In your most recent position, what problems have you identified that had previously been overlooked?

Keep your answer brief and do not brag unduly.

40. If you had your choice of jobs or companies, where would you choose?

Talk about the job at hand and what is attractive in the company that is interviewing you.

41. Why are you not earning more at your age?

Do not be defensive about this. Explain that you are hoping to correct the situation through this career change.

42. What do you feel you should earn in the proposed position?

You may want to answer this question as follows: 'What is the typical salary range for similar jobs in your company?" If there is no range in the company, give the range that you had in mind. But qualify it by saying you hope to learn more about the job responsibilities and scope.

43. If we were to offer you this position, exactly how much would you expect?

Again, be careful about pinning yourself down – either too high or too low if possible; deal in terms of what the market value is for the job. For example, "My understanding is that a job like this which you are describing might well pay in the range of £xx to £xx. How does this fit with the present salary structure?"

44. Do you have any objections to taking a battery of psychological tests?

No, none at all (this would mean you are a serious candidate).

45. What other types of jobs or companies are you considering at this time?

Do not feel obliged to reveal details of your other negotiations. If you have other irons in the fire, refer to your campaign in a general way, but concentrate mainly on the job at hand.

46. What sort of outside reading do you do?

Be honest. If possible, mention some of the things you read in order to keep yourself up to date in your professional field. However, it is fitting to show balanced interests by your recreational reading as well.

47. Do you consider yourself to be a creative person?

Yes (and be prepared to give a couple of examples).

48. How would you describe your own personality?

Balanced and human. Mention two or three useful traits.

49. Are you a leader?

Yes (give examples).

50. What are your long-range goals?

Relate your answer to the company you are interviewing with, rather than giving a very broad general answer. Keep your ambitions on a realistic track.

51. What are your strongest points?

Be ready to present at least three – preferably in a way that relates them to the potential job opening.

52. How long would you expect to stay with our company?

You can hedge a little here while saying that you would expect: (1) to progress with your new company, and (2)that salary would keep up with this progress, as well as inflation.

If you are pressed, you might answer that ten years might well bring a doubling of salary for a person who is moving well within his company.

53. What sort of relationship do you have with your associates, at the same level and above and below you?

This is a very important question, and you can afford to take your time and answer it in steps.

When talking about your relationships with subordinates, be prepared to state your philosophy of handling them, particularly when they have performance problems.

With regard to bosses, indicate your keen interest in understanding the expectations of your boss, so that you and your organisation can build your goals in a way that will support his goals. You may also want to talk about how you would go about keeping your boss informed.

54. What are some of your activities or recreations?

Your answer can show that you lead a balanced life. But avoid throwing in so many outside activities that it casts some doubt on how much time you will have for your job. Remember, too, that your hobbies and recreations can be quite revealing as to your own personality.

55. Are you continuing your education?

If you are not actually attending or planning to attend formal classes, be ready to explain what sort of outside reading or attendance at professional seminars you undertake in order to keep yourself fresh in your chosen field.

UNIT 42: INTERVIEWS – FROM THE EMPLOYER'S PERSPECTIVE

Prospective employers, as you will readily appreciate, are fully aware that a CV will have been prepared to highlight the applicant's suitability to the vacant position. The written word, however, is no substitute for a face-to-face meeting at interview.

In my experience, there have been so many occasions where the interviewee has not reflected the mental picture conjured up from the application letter and CV. In such circumstances, the effects can be either positive or negative and therefore it is so important that the CV is an accurate summary of *you*.

Preparation

I like an applicant to be well prepared for the interview and as relaxed as possible. Here are some suggestions:

- Research your prospective employer and gain as much knowledge as you can about the business, its ethics, its market position and how it differentiates itself from its competitors. Most of all, gain a comprehensive understanding of the business and try to imagine the attributes it might be seeking from its employees.

- Thoroughly review your CV.

- Have a list of questions you might wish to ask.

- Wear the type of clothing which mirrors the job you are applying for. Try to find at least one piece of clothing which makes you feel good.

- Leave home in plenty of time and allow for travel hiccups. You will have arrived early, so check on where you should report and, time allowing, have a coffee or a short walk.

- As best as possible, relax. Remember that being relaxed will show the real you.

The Interview

First impressions are important. Be confident, but don't appear cocky. Give a warm smile rather than a forced smile. Feel pleased to be where you are. Remember what was said previously about body language and mirroring the interviewer.

Don'ts

- Don't be long-winded in response to questions. Be concise, clear and stick to the point. If you are not clear as to what is being asked, then request clarification. **Once you have lost the attention of the interviewer it is very difficult to regain it.**

- Don't be afraid of admitting that you don't know the answer to a question. Honesty is the best policy and fluffing an answer is far worse than admitting that you don't have an answer.

- Don't name-drop. There is no need for this and it can be a turn-off.

- Don't criticise former employers in any way.

- Don't appear over confident. This can be just as bad as being a shrinking violet.

- Don't appear over familiar. Tend towards the more formal approach.

- Don't express opinions which might be deemed controversial or inappropriate.

Dos

- Do thank the interviewer for the opportunity of progressing your job application

- Do remember that the interviewer is not there to trick you; he/she wants to know about YOU, to confirm your skills and to identify how you might match the requirements of the job for which you are applying, and the culture of the business. Be honest.

- Be aware of the interviewer's body language.

- Do show keen interest in the prospective employer's business by asking just one or two intelligent questions if the opportunity arises. Have these questions well prepared, and ensure that they are not already in the public domain.

- Listen very carefully to questions being asked.

- Try and enjoy the interview process, both as a learning process and as an opportunity of meeting new people.

Summary

Remember having a major impact re FIRST IMPRESSIONS. Practise what should be a standard opening to any interview, ie; arrival, introductions etc. Be confident and relaxed and stay marginally on the plus side of formality.

Remember that your CV was the selling document, the interview is a sampling of the product. All you can do is give of your best on the day and be honest.

Do try to enjoy the experience and....and the experience and opportunity will deliver what you truly want!

UNIT 43: THE TOP10 POWER QUESTIONS

AndrewSobel, co-author of *Power Questions: Build Relationships, Win New Business, and Influence Others*

If you talk to recruiters and executives who are actively hiring, they will tell you that there are three types of questions they get: none, bad ones, and— very rarely— memorable ones. And the candidates who ask the memorable ones are often the ones they make offers to. "You'd be surprised," a recruiter for a fast-growing technology company told me, "how many job candidates have absolutely no questions for me at all, or they ask dumb or boring questions like 'so what do you do?'".

You want a recruiter or executive who interviews you to tell a colleague afterwards, "I had a great conversation with that candidate. He had really thought a lot about our business". That's what gets you the call-back. And good questions are the way you create a thought-provoking, value-added conversation.

First, avoid these types of questions in a job interview:

- Informational questions. Don't take up a manager's time asking "How much vacation will I get?" *Get the basic information you need before you go in for an interview.*

- Closed-ended questions. If someone can give a 'yes' or 'no' answer, it diminishes your prospects for having a good conversation.

- 'Me' questions. An executive is interested in how you will add value to their organisation and whether or not you're a good fit. Skip questions like "I skydive every Saturday—so will I ever be asked to work weekends?"

Here are the kinds of questions you should be asking in a job interview:

1. Credibility-building questions: "As I think back to my experience in managing large sales forces, I've found there are typically three barriers to breakthrough sales performance: coordination of the sales function with marketing and manufacturing; customer selection; and product quality. I'm curious, what would you say are the main factors that have been responsible for your own lack of sales growth?"

2. 'Why?' questions: "Why did you close down your parts business rather than try to find a buyer for it?" or "Why did you decide to move from a functional to a product- based organization structure?"

3. Personal understanding questions: "I understand you joined the organisation five years ago. With all the growth you've had, how do you find the experience of working here now compared to when you started?"

4. Passion questions: "What do you love most about working here?"

5. Value-added advice questions: "Have you considered creating an online platform for your top account executives from around the world to share success stories and collaborate around key client opportunities? We implemented such a concept a year ago and it's been very successful"

6. Future-oriented questions: "You've achieved large increases in productivity over the last three years. Where do you believe future operational improvements will come from?"

7. Aspiration questions: "As you look ahead to the next couple of years, what are the potential growth areas that people are most excited about in the company?"

8. Organizational culture questions: "What are the most common reasons why new employees don't work out here?"

9. Decision-making questions: "If we were to arrive at two final candidates with equal experience and skills, how would you choose one over the other?"

10. Company strengths-and-weaknesses questions: "Why do people come to work for you rather than a competitor?" And then, "Why do you think they stay?"

If you want to be noticed by recruiters, don't talk more—ask better questions.

UNIT 44: FOLLOW UP THAT INTERVIEW - IF SUCCESSFUL

Okay, so you have secured your 'Dream Job' - what next – it is not quite over yet. Get In and Fit In!

Step 1
You receive that telephone call to say that you have been accepted for the position subject to satisfactory references. They state that they will put this in writing and check with you the correct contact details of your references. Remember you have these on a separate attached sheet to your CV. Make sure email address and contact numbers are there including mobile number.

You thank them and await letter of confirmation.

Step 2
Your Letter of Confirmation arrives stating start date, time and venue and who to report to.

You send them a Letter of Confirmation.

Step 3
In preparation for your first day in the new job, check your Transport, Wardrobe, Parking etc.

Step 4
Arrive early for your Induction which may be over a period of one to three days.

Step 5
Your Contract and Probation Period is normally 6 months – remember that!

Step 6
LISTEN and LEARN.

Step 7
Stay focused, be polite and accommodating and *Go That Extra Mile*!

Step 8
Arrive early and stay late – do not clock-watch.

Step 9
Take work home if needed – but anyway, always go home and further research your work and come back for that the next day with new information.

Step 10
Attend all meetings – even those out of hours.

Step 11
Attend all other events – show interest.

Step 12
Don't step on others' toes – be part of that team – but slowly show initiative.

Step 13
Always be aware of your Job Specification and nail those points.

Step 14

Know who makes the decisions – who shouts the loudest – who really counts and be aware of internal politics and pecking order.

Step 15

Find your feet – feel your way around slowly but surely – Strategy – influence!

Step 16

Analyse the skills of the team and see where you fit in and where the strengths and weaknesses lie. If a weakness in the team is IT – you upgrade your IT Skills and show an interest in this and ask the company to invest in these skills for the benefit of the company and the team.

Step 17

Do not get involved in internal gossip – do not take sides and do not gang up on others.

Step 18

No sickness – no holidays.

Step 19

Be Punctual.

Step 20

After 6 months, prepare your Strategy demonstrating what you have achieved in relation to the job specification and take this to your Appraisal – then prepare your next 6 month Strategy.

Step 21

Focus on your own Personal Development within the structure of the organisation and where you want to be in 12 months from now and how you will get there.

UNIT 45: FOLLOW UP THAT INTERVIEW - IF NOT SUCCESSFUL

If you receive confirmation that you have been unsuccessful by whatever means: letter, email, text, phone, in person or via third parties - always ask for feedback.

Please do not take it personally – this feedback is supposed to be positive, objective criticism and should highlight those areas you need to work on.

Common points raised:

- Did not have enough experience
- Did not have as much experience as other candidates
- Other candidates had more IT system knowledge.

Sometimes these points act as a polite way of saying they just preferred someone else.

Whatever they quote, though, please act on it for next time. So if CRM systems keep coming up time and time again, then enrol on a course to rectify this problem.

In this economic climate most state that the calibre of candidates was exceptional and it was very hard to come to a decision, so please take this that you were suitable – but remember *Rapport* - someone who was going to be working with you may have felt that they could work with someone else with more ease.

So, you were not UNSUCCESSFUL– you just cannot win the award for the most likeable person all the time!

Recovery time

If they have congratulated you on a polished interview, then you are doing the right thing and it is only a matter of time before you will 'Nail That Job'.

Move on and get back in that driving seat and get back to your Job Search Strategy. This should be done immediately!

If you are devastated, then you need to get over it and move on – some personal coaches/mentors would encourage you to challenge this decision – though personally the ONLY thing I would do is to practise my interview techniques.

Speak to the person who made the decision and express your ongoing interest in the role and ask to be kept on file for the future – in case the new person does not survive their Probation Period and other vacancies may come up within the organisation that you might be suitable for.

Then bring this to a Close and move on to Better and Bigger Things!

Exercise- Questions asked at interview

- "Do you wear 'wellies' and what size do you take?"

This question took me totally off-guard and I answered half of it:"Yes, I do possess 'wellies' – why?"

This question still baffles me and fills me with humour though I did not ask the interviewer the significance of this. However the 'wellie' question remains a mystery to me and what would be your Amswer and what would be your interpretation of this Question?

UNIT 46: CHECKLIST ACTION PLAN – PREPARATION FOR AN INTERVIEW

STEPS	ACTIONS	DOs	DON'Ts	RESULT
1	Confirmation	Reciprocate	Ignore	
2	Research	Web/Employees	Make assumptions	
3	Positive thinking	You want the job	What if	
4	Impress	Immaculate dress/firm handshake/ eye contact	Shabby appearance/limp handshake	
5	Preparation	Knowledge/Experience	Leave to last minute	
6	Revise	Company's objectives	Assume	
7	Relax	Breathing techniques	Panic	
8	Early bird	Arrive 15 minutes early	Be late	
9	Body language	Upright/Proud	Irritating habits	
10	Impact	Impress from start to finish	Inconsistent	
11	Sell yourself	Reinforce positive thinking	Weak answers	

301

12	Timing	Be aware of time	Waffle on
13	Influence and persuade	You are the one for the job	Take your eyes off the objective
14	Establish rapport	Likeability	Create an atmosphere
15	Pace	Have a flow	Be stuck for answers
16	Q/A	Clear and concise	Negative/not knowing
17	Examples/evidence	Past work experience	Ramble
18	Listen	At all times	Confirm questions
19	Fitting in	Image/branding observation	Ignore corporate image
20	Interviewer's needs	Not personal needs	List your personal needs
21	Power questions	1-3 questions, personal development	No mention of money, time off, holidays or breaks etc.
22	Closure	They end interview	You talk on
23	Lasting impression	Firm handshake/eye contact	Forget to say thank you

UNIT 47: TOP 10 JOBS FOR 2013

A potential occupation's responsibilities, salary, opportunity, and training are vitael in a job search. But then there are other crucial components that keep us coming to work every day. Are the job's tasks what you expected? Do you have room to broaden your skills and build a career? Are you having trouble setting boundaries between your personal time and professional life? You don't want to accept a job that sounded good in the listing and in the interview, but that then starts to smell funny once you're up close and in the office.

Our tastes in what we like to do and how we like to work are all distinctive, so it's tough to quantify them to determine the better occupations. Still, this year's picks and rankings do take into account the day-to-day of a profession. As an example, Nelly Yusupova, the Chief Technology Officer of Webgrsls International, says workplaces for Web Developers run the gamut "from a very flexible, hands on, nimble, 'fly by the seat of your pants' environment of a startup and [being] very involved with every aspect of a project, to a very structured environment with more levels of approval and a more bureaucratic approach with limited responsibilities". When a Web Developer's sometimes fluid, sometimes chaotic work environment was weighed along with the job's competitive salary, unemployment rate, excellent job prospects, and projected growth, the occupation placed ninth on our list of Best Jobs.

By comparison, a restaurant cook (our No. 81 pick) has to consider the tense and hot atmosphere of a commercial kitchen, plus the number of hours and weekends devoted to the work. But on the plus side, they'll also find it's a job with good prospects, plus a decent growth and employment rate.

Here are the top 10 jobs of 2013:

1. Dentist
2. Registered Nurse
3. Pharmacist
4. Computer Systems Analyst
5. Physician
6. Database Administrator
7. Software Developer
8. Physical Therapist
9. Web Developer
10. Dental Hygienist

From completing our Transferable Skills Exercises you should be able to see if you have the skills to cross over to one of the above jobs if you want to change?

I had a stress massage today, and I asked for a tip on what to do to solve my problem - change your job - so looking at the above - I decided on ….?

UNIT 48: HOW TO VALUE YOUR PERFORMANCE AT INTERVIEW

You can rate your own Interview Performance using a scoring system 1-10 with 10 being highest. If you score below 8 on any, then you did not deserve that job, so practise until you score 10 in all areas and then you know you own that job and deserve it!

Research
Did you demonstrate your knowledge about the company? Research format of interview.

Questions/answers
How well did you respond to the questions? Did you give examples? Could you have done better?

Rapport with the interviewer(s)
Did you engage in polite conversation? Were you at ease – did you make them feel comfortable?

Your questions
Were your questions sensible, knowledgeable and asked with enthusiasm? Did you have eye contact with the person who asked you a question?

Follow up that interview

Did you send that letter/email and reinforce your good points?

RESEARCH	Q/A	RAPPORT	YOUR QUESTIONS	FOLLOW UP	TOTAL

UNIT 49: PROBATIONARY PERIOD ONCE YOU'VE NAILED THAT JOB

You're about to start a new job and decide to read through your Employment Contract for the first time. Is there a surer way to tarnish your early enthusiasm and optimism than realising that you will have to work through a probationary period before becoming a full employee? Learning that early failure to perform may mean you're given less than one week's notice leaves you feeling like anything but a valuable new member of the team. Why wasn't this mentioned at the interview stage?

It's a common element of most employment contracts

In fact, you should never be surprised to learn that you will be on probation for the first few weeks or months with a new employer. Firstly, most firms require that you serve a probationary period. Secondly, you should always read your Employment Contract before accepting any offer, so there should be no room for shocking realisations at any later stage. Armed with the knowledge that you should expect to find a probation paragraph in your contract, you should be ready to recognise and deal with any deviations from the norm.

How long do they last?

Probationary periods usually last for three months. Some employers will be happy to take you on as a full employee after only a few days; others will require you to work for a whole year before you satisfy their requirements. Next, you need to know how much notice of termination of employment is required on each side. In the majority of cases this will be one week. If the normal terms of your contract would require three months' notice on both sides, then probationary notice may be one month or more. In some cases, there may be an asymmetry in the notice required by either side. For example, you may have to give your employer a week's notice, while they are only obliged to tell you the day before, or vice-versa.

What about salary, absence or sickness?

Pay attention to what will happen to your remuneration while on probation - will you be obliged to accept a lower starting salary for a few weeks? Will your commission from sales be lower than that of someone who has successfully completed their probation period? What about absence due to sickness? In each case, you must scrutinise your contract before putting your name to this legally binding document. There may be occasions where your particular requirements are not covered in the contract, for example, the question of whether or not maternity leave is dealt with in the same way while on probation. Make sure that you ask for such to be clarified in your Terms of Employment before committing yourself. This section of your contract is, in many ways, a self-contained Employment Contract in itself and so deserves close attention.

Getting through it

We'll assume that you are now over the shock of having to work a probationary period and all the implications that has for your job security, salary, benefits and so on. How do you ensure that you get through the next weeks and months without any problems? At this point, it's useful to remember that this clause in your contract works both ways - your employer is on probation too. Do not fall into the trap that you must endure everything that is thrown at you because your primary aim is to get through the next three months. If your employer does not come up to scratch, it's time to think about making the most of the shortened notice period part of your contract - your boss is bound by its terms too.

Dos and Don'ts

What if you actually like your new job, you get on with your colleagues, the canteen serves a variety of excellent dishes and the commute home is bearable? How do you ensure that they'll want to keep you on once your probationary period has expired? Or, to turn that around, what sort of behaviour is likely to get you ejected? Poor timekeeping is a sure way to make your boss feel that he or she has made a poor decision in hiring you. Even if everybody else in your department staggers in at 10:30, you should make a special effort to arrive in good time because somebody will be watching and noting your behaviour.

Failure to get to grips with the basic skills and routines of your post are a certain way to get the sack. The details of these requirements may not have been obvious when you applied for the job. For example, your employer may assume that you are an experienced user of Microsoft Word, Excel and PowerPoint. Many people have found themselves being shown the door after displaying spectacular ignorance of office technology - be sure that you can compose and send email, resize windows and turn the monitor on/off if your new place of work depends on IT. The mouse should not be used as a foot pedal.

Cuts both ways

However, there is a flipside to all of this. It is your employer's responsibility to take all reasonable steps to help you through your probation period, to provide any and all training, mentoring and encouragement that you need. Once again, remember that they too are on probation. I have seen a particularly good Employment Contract that requires that the content of one's final probationary assessment should not contain any surprises. If criticism of your performance is contained in the final report then it must only be included as a summary and re-assertion of what has been said before. The same contract also states that the employer is responsible for keeping one informed of one's progress or any lack thereof. Having a clause like this in your own contract is something worth fighting for.

When it's complete

What are the possible outcomes once the completion date arrives? In many cases, your boss will call you into the office to inform you that everything is satisfactory or one morning you may find a Confirmation of Completion document on your desk. If you have really shone, if your performance has exceeded everybody's expectations, you may even be offered a promotion (which may or may not come with its own probationary period).

Sometimes, a worker's performance may fall a little short of the target. In this case, it's possible that the period will be extended for another month or so or until the employer is satisfied that all the requirements have been met. Alternatively, a worker who has demonstrably failed to be up to the job may be moved sideways or downwards to another position. The worst case, of course, is being asked to leave during or at the completion of one's probationary period. If this happens to you, be aware that since 1999 employees in the United Kingdom can only make a claim for unfair dismissal after twelve months of continuous employment (before 1999 it was two years). Other countries have stricter employment laws. For example, a recent case in New Zealand saw a successful claim for unfair dismissal even though the claimant had only been employed for 32 hours. The Commission ordered compensation equivalent to four months' salary on the basis that the employee was 'ready, willing and able to perform tasks'. It turned out that the employer had never issued a written confirmation of the employee's probationary period.

Finally, if you yourself decide that your employer has not met your targets and left you feeling unwelcome and undervalued (perhaps by failing to provide interesting work or proper support and training), you must give proper notice that you intend to terminate your employment. We always recommend that you do this in the correct way and abide by the terms of your Employment Contract with style and dignity: arrange a meeting with your boss in which you should explain your reasons for leaving before handing over an appropriate letter of resignation. If nothing else, this approach will make it more likely that this employer provides your next employer with a favourable reference.

UNIT 50: ENTPREPRENEURIAL MIND SET

From my own personal experience, back in the last recession, I turned my life around and had started two businesses: **Gold Introductions** – a Social Networking Agency, which featured on TV, radio and in various magazines; and **Advanced Training**, which secured many contracts with London - LETEC,BGCC,CONNEXIONS, Brighton University – and many more.

So, in times of economic downturn and you find yourself without a job – this could be the excuse you have been looking for:

Having found myself in a similar situation again in 2009 I started www.ccoworkcic.com and then went on in 2011 to establish www.workbizacademy.co.uk. This year (2013)I am franchising CCO WORK CIC and turning the programmes into E-Learning Programmes; in 2014 I will launch a new online upmarket travel www.dolcevitaescapes.com - a new Community Start Up Program - THE GATEWAY and so much more. Perhaps that BB by the seaside which is on my list.

I am also delivering Graduate Programmes in Hope University and Manchester Innovation Centre and am a Lead Partner for the NW/NE for the Rockstar Youth Group supporting the Start-Up Programmes with mentoring and workshops.

Turn Your Hobby Into a Business

Okay – you have an IDEA – maybe it is a hobby of yours which you can turn into a profitable business.

Example

One of our members came to us - Steven - after being made redundant from a large telecommunications company after 30 years as a Senior Director. He had quite a considerable redundancy payment and wanted to start a Bird Sanctuary with it. We explored this idea with him and then we found out his other passion was racing road bikes. He now has one of the most successful bike shops in the North West.

Are you BORN an ENTREPRENEUR or can you become one?

A few years ago I would have endorsed that you are born an Entrepreneur, but in 2013 I started working on the 18-30 Rock Star Youth Start-Up Programme www.rockstaryouth.co.uk and through delivering the Incubators I have realised that you can train, educate and lead an entrepreneur mind-set. We have £10k per person re: a loan with free mentoring support and expertise support via events, workshops and e-learning. So with this crutch - how could you fail?

Before you start - DOYOUR HOMEWORK:

Competitors

Who are your competitors? Research them and find out who they are and what they do and whether you can compete or offer another service/product at a more competitive price and better quality.

It's good to talk

Network and talk to people in your industry to avoid the unnecessary pitfalls and find out what would be the potential start up problems. Read: *Making It* by Lou Gimson and Allison Mitchell.

Can you turn a hobby into a business?

Fitness fanatic? – register at www.excerciseregister.org ;

- Making home-made beauty products - abide by EU regulations;
- Cookery - contact your local Council for Food and Hygiene courses;

Jewellery design - see your local University for courses or visit www.bja.org.uk.

Business mentor/coach

You may need someone to mentor you who has been in business before, or you may want a mentor who can work with you on:

- personal assertiveness
- the power of negotiation
- no hardball tactics.

This is not a hostile role but an interactive role to try to understand the needs of the person or business.

Set boundaries Decide on your lower and upper limits - then you know what to expect and what to build upon and when to walk away.

Define your relationship - Do not make it personal as they could use these details to exploit you. Distance yourself – it is a business relationship, not a friendship.

Research

Know what the company are paying and what they get for this – though value your service or goods.

Once your Research / Consultation / Feasibility Study has been completed then you can collate this information into a Business Plan.

Business Plan checklist: - What should your business plan try to include?

- **Business Objectives**

  Describe your short, medium and long-term objectives, showing what you want to achieve with your business.

- **Management**

  Highlight the work experience, education and qualifications of the Key People that will be relevant to your business, e.g. book-<u>keeping</u> experience, industry experience etc. (possibly a CV if you have one).

- **Premises**

  Describe your choice of business premises, including size, location, state of repair and full associated costs. Try to explain why you chose the premises, showing any competitive advantage it may offer.

- **Plant, machinery and equipment**

  Detail any existing plant, machinery and equipment you own, showing any outstanding finance and present value. Detail any plant, machinery and equipment you propose to purchase in the future including estimated prices.

- **Products and services**

  Describe in detail the main products and services offered by your business, going into enough detail so that someone with no knowledge of your type of business will be able to understand what you are doing. What is unique about your particular products and services?

- **Pricing your product or service**

  Describe how you arrived at the price for your product or service. Give a sample of the price(s) you will charge or do charge, showing how your prices compare with your competitors'.

- **Customers and markets**

  Show who, where and how many potential customers you have (locally, regionally or nationally if appropriate). Outline any marketing research that you have done that demonstrates a demand for your product, including any information on your competitors.

- **Promotion**

  Describe in detail what level of sales you anticipate, showing any firm orders in hand. Also explain what assumptions have been made in making your sales forecast, how you intend to market and advertise your products and services, and why you believe your sales forecasts are realistic.

- **Financial information**

  Start-up businesses - Financial projections (at least a cash-flow) for your business, including notes, explaining your projections.

  Existing businesses - As above, but please include any Annual Accounts or Management Information you might also possess.

If you are looking to start a business or have started and then funding and mentoring support then log on now to join us on our UK Roadshow and attend one of our Incubator Days www.rockstaryouth.co.uk will support you with a Business Plan/Cash Flow and so much more.

UNIT 51: NOW YOU HAVE THE JOB YOU DESERVE!

You have now worked your way through this book, which is based on a Programme I deliver at present for the Conservative Association campaign – **'Get Britain Working** 'in the North West (Warrington). It is a bespoke ten-week training course based on the accreditation by ILM Level 3/7 Leadership & Management which has been designed to enable participants to take responsibility for their own destination and move forward, onwards and upwards. Free newsletter and updates are available at: www.ccoworkcic.com.

It is only through having worked in this industry and assisting people who are unemployed for over 20 years; working through yet another recession, being unemployed myself and currently assisting family members who are unemployed, that I decided to produce this book so that it becomes your bible and guidance until you nail that dream job!

This model works. On my first pilot of running a course based on this book I achieved 11 out of 13 into employment and continue with a 75% overall success rate. Now, having run the above programmes for over 5 years and being onto our

13th programme, we have the magic formula. It is true that it is a science and each of these Units is complimented with a Digital Workshop - that is what has changed in finding work.

Through our Programmes we have placed over 800 people into employment and over 400 people into self employment over the last six years - so this formula does work - try it!

There are some key factors that if you follow this book you will:

Have the tools to confidently go out there in the present job market and nail that DREAM JOB:

- Learn new skills –e.g. e-marketing – a must in this economic climate;

- Re-gain your confidence – become positive and assertive in this Job Market;

- Learn to evaluate your transferable skills – in order to have a career change if needed;

- Learn to value yourself, your skills and your experience and showcase these to perspective employers.

If you want this – TAKE ACTION – and it will become a reality. Believe me – if I can do it – so can you!

The fact that you got this far tells me that you are raring to go.

I have already given you tools for a Weekly/Daily Action Plan in Unit 35, and a one to twelve week Employment Strategy in Unit 36 – so here we go!

Goal Setting – Achieving your Aims and Objectives

You have the TOOLS - I want you to aim high and just be prepared to go all the way to the top.

You will know whether to:

- Continue on the same career path;
- Have a career change – through acknowledging your transferable skills;
- Start your own business.

If you follow this guide, working your way through this book you will, sooner rather than later, receive that Job Offer.

Don't delay – do it now – and you will feel much more fulfilled.

ABOUT THE AUTHOR

Karen Melonie Gould Director of www.ccoworkcic.com is presently the Director NW/NE for the Start Up Loans Government Program through www.rockstaryouth.co.uk

Karen is an ILM Fellow who delivers to Level 7 Leadership and Management – CMI – CIPD and has a Masters in Business Administration. CCO WORK CIC is presently delivering a Level 2/5 Leadership and Management Programs in Warrington.

Karen has worked Internationally from USA to the Caribbean to Europe and beyond and has also worked in London with the Top FTSE Companies re Employability for Graduates and Leadership and Management/Mentoring Programs for Executives using Training/Mentoring from Price Waterhouse to Kleinwort Benson etc.

Karen lives in Chester with her husband who is a local Chef and she enjoys in her spare time, ZUMBA, Dancing and Pilates. Karen sits on the local LEP STRATEGY Boards for Employment, Business Start Ups and Growth. Karen is a local Accelerator Growth Coach. Karen enjoys travelling and exploring new and exciting international cuisine and places of beauty. Walking and water sports are a keen passion of hers. Karen enjoys Fashion and socialising with her friends. Karen has run the Warrington Work and Business Club since 2006 for David Mowat MP for Warrington South on a voluntary basis and has a great Team of Mentors to support her.

Karen enjoys life to the full as Business Mentor working with over 100 Young Entrepreneurs, sourcing businesses for Growth to prepare for Growth Funding and is a Business Angel NW. Karen, herself is a true Entrepreneur and 'talent spotter' and has indeed, invested herself in new and exciting businesses for the future.